"LANGUAGE" IN INDIAN PHILOSOPHY AND RELIGION

edited and introduced by

HAROLD G. COWARD

SUPPLEMENTS / 5

X

"LANGUAGE" IN INDIAN PHILOSOPHY AND RELIGION

Edited and Introduced by

Harold G. Coward

University of Calgary

Canadian Cataloguing in Publication Data

Main entry under title:

Language in Indian philosophy and religion

(SR supplements ; 5)

Papers originally read at a seminar sponsored by the Canadian Society for the Study of Religion/ Société canadienne des sciences religieuses at Laval University, Quebec City, Quebec, May 28th to 30th, 1976.

Includes index.
ISBN 0-919812-07-4 pa.

1. Philosophy, Indic - Congresses. 2. Languages - Philosophy - Congresses. I. Coward, Harold G., 1936- II. Canadian Society for the Study of Religion. III. Series.

B131.L35 181'.4 C77-001780-0

To Professor T.R.V. Murti

CONTENTS

EDITORIAL NOTE viii

ABOUT THE AUTHORS ix

HAROLD G. COWARD / Introduction 1

KLAUS KLOSTERMAIER / The Creative Function of the Word 5

KRISHNA SIVARAMAN / The Saiva and the Grammarian Perspectives of Language 19

DEBABRATA SINHA / Reflections on Some Key Terms in Advaita Vedānta 33

MERVYN SPRUNG / Non-Cognitive Language in Mādhyamika Buddhism 43

BIMAL KRISHNA MATILAL / The Ineffable 55

MAHESH MEHTA / Ineffability Reconsidered 63

LESLIE KAWAMURA / Is Reconstruction from Tibetan into Sanskrit Possible? 83

EDITORIAL NOTE

The papers published in this volume were originally read and discussed at a three day seminar sponsored by the Canadian Society for the Study of Religion/Societie Canadienne des Sciences Religieuses at Laval University, Quebec City, Quebec, May 28th to 30th, 1976. This seminar served the important function of bringing together the majority of the Canadian scholars who specialize in Indian Philosophy and Religion. The topic, *Language*, was chosen a year earlier so that advance study on a common theme could be undertaken by all who participated. Some thirty professors, as well as a few senior graduate students, engaged in the discussion. An additional and important feature of the seminar was that since it was held during the Learned Societies meetings, a number of Western scholars with an interest in language were able to listen in to the thinking of their Eastern colleagues. This provided the basis for some interesting and informed dialogue.

In addition to those whose papers are printed in this volume, the seminar benefited from the following scholars who acted as formal respondents: Roy Amore, University of Windsor; Terence Day, University of Manitoba; Leon Hurvitz, University of British Columbia; and Wayne Whillier, McMaster University.

A special word of thanks is due to Penny Rusk, Carolina Maloney and Joan Barton, secretaries in the office of the Department of Religious Studies, University of Calgary, for their patient typing and retyping of the manuscripts until a camera-ready copy was achieved. Finally, as organizer and chairman of the seminar, I want to acknowledge the support given this project by Cathleen Going, Past President of CSSR, and the encouragement of Peter Slater, CSSR Publications Officer, to assemble this volume for the Mini-Publication Series of the society.

October, 1976

Harold G. Coward
Department of Religious Studies
The University of Calgary
Calgary, Alberta
Canada

ABOUT THE AUTHORS

HAROLD COWARD is Associate Professor and Head of the Department of Religious Studies at the University of Calgary, Calgary, Alberta, Canada. He holds a Ph.D. in Indian Philosophy and Religion from McMaster University. In 1972, he was a visiting scholar at Banaras Hindu University, Varanasi, India. His essays and reviews have appeared in The Philosophical Quarterly (India), The Journal of the American Academy of Religion, The Journal for the Scientific Study of Religion, and Studies In Religion. He is the author of Bhartrhari (1976), and editor of Mystics and Scholars (1977).

LESLIE KAWAMURA is Assistant Professor of Religious Studies at the University of Calgary, Calgary, Alberta, Canada. He holds a Ph.D. in Tibetan Buddhism from the University of Saskatchewan and an M.A. from Kyoto University, Japan. He is co-author with Herbert Guenther of Mind In Buddhist Psychology (1975), and author of the Golden Zepher (1975)

KLAUS KLOSTERMAIER is Professor of Religious Studies at the University of Manitoba, Winnipeg, Manitoba, Canada. He holds a Dr. Phil. in Philosophy from the Gregorian University, Rome and a Ph.D. in Ancient Indian History and Culture from Bombay University, and studied and taught in India for nine years. He is the author of Hinduismus (1965), Hindu and Christian in Vrindaban (1970), Mahatma Gandhi: Freiheit ohne Gewalt (1968) Salvation, Liberation, Self-realization (1974) and numerous articles in Orientalist and Philosophical and Religious Studies Journals.

BIMAL KRISHNA MATILAL is Spaulding Professor of Comparative Religion, Oxford University. He previously taught in the Department of Sanskrit and Indian Studies, University of Toronto. He is editor of the Journal of Indian Philosophy, and author of Epistemology, Logic and Grammar in Indian Philosophical Analysis (1971) and The Navya-nyāya Doctrine of Negation (1968).

ABOUT THE AUTHORS

MAHESH MEHTA is Associate Professor of Indian and Buddhist Philosophy and Religion at the University of Windsor. He holds a Ph.D. from Bombay University and studied and taught at the Universities of Bombay, Pennsylvania and Windsor for ten years. He is the author of "The Mahābhārata - A Study of the Critical Edition (in press)

DEBARATA SINHA is Professor of Philosophy at Brock University, St. Catherines, Ontario, Canada. He holds a Ph.D. from Calcutta University.

KRISHNA SIVARAMAN is Associate Professor of Religion at McMaster University, Hamilton, Ontario, Canada. He holds a Ph.D. from Banaras Hindu University where he taught before coming to Canada. He is author of Saivism in Philosophical Perspective (1972).

MERVYN SPRUNG is Professor of Philosophy at Brock University, St. Catherines, Ontario, Canada. He holds a Ph.D. from Berlin. His published articles have appeared in various Philosophy and Religious Studies journals. He is the editor of The Problem of Two Truths in Buddhism and Vedanta (1973).

INTRODUCTION

By Harold Coward

The papers contained in this volume not only present the ongoing debate over language in Indian thought, but they also relate at key points to the discussion of language in contemporary Western philosophy. This should prove helpful to Western scholars venturing forth into Indian philosophy for the first time. For the Eastern specialists themselves, the references to modern Western thinking on language are suggestive of comparative studies that should be undertaken in the future. Since these essays were composed under the time and space limitations of a conference, they make no pretense at exhausting the discussion of language in Indian thought - no three day seminar could do that! Yet, within this limitation, many of the key problems regarding language are effectively examined.

Klaus Klostermaier takes us far back into traditional Indian thought and introduces the thesis of the Grammarian School, namely, that language or word has the power to create and reveal reality. He helpfully distinguishes the positive connotation of the term *creative* in the West from the Indian notion of creation as but a retracing of the forgotten eternal truth. As Klostermaier puts it, whereas creation in the West is like the making of a *new* path, the great Indian thinkers describe their activity and the function of language as the clearing of an overgrown ancient path so as to return or rediscover the source. He also introduces the very broad and many-sided manner in which the terms *language* and *word* are used in Indian thought. Although this way of thinking of language is not common in the West, Klostermaier points out that it is found in Hebrew and Christian sources. In addition to presenting in a clear way the philosophy of language of the Grammarians, Klostermaier's paper provides interesting comparisons between this ancient Indian viewpoint and the theories of modern physics and biology. He argues that both modern science and the ancient Indian view of language share a common theoretical position; namely, that the relationship between reality and thought is not one of simple identity or difference, but rather a *symmetry* correlating two realities that mutually constitute each other.

In his paper Krishna Sivaraman welcomes the Grammarian theory of language, but, in true Indian fashion, he argues that the Grammarian view has a major weakness which is corrected by the Śaiva approach. The point at issue is this. Whereas for the Grammarian the ultimate or absolute is language itself (*śabdabrahman*), for the Śaiva philosopher language is not ultimate but simply a power of the ultimate, i.e., *parama śiva*. Language in the Śaiva approach, therefore, is not to be viewed as an independent self-subsistent principle - the way it is conceived within the Grammar School. The Saiva view is that language or speech is not itself *being* but only an actualization of being. As Sivaraman concludes, "It is the difference between achieving transcendence *in* language and the achieving of transcendence of language itself."

As Debabrata Sinha points out, Advaita Vedānta, like Saivism, looks for a reality beyond language itself. The issue is one that is shared by modern approaches to the philosophy of language. How far can language be taken as an expression of reality? Since in most Eastern viewpoints one must trust some form of direct intuition for the experience of reality, Sinha examines the techniques of the Upanisadic seers in which language is often used in a negative way to clear the ground for intuition. Before presenting the Advaita Vedānta solution to the problem of bridging the gap between language and reality, Sinha notes the inferential approaches of recent Western thinkers such as Russell, and Wittgenstein, and the Indian Nyāya school. In the Advaita view although the ultimate reality is beyond language, language participates in that ultimate. The relation between the two is neither complete identity nor complete difference. Sinha suggests that language has the symbolic function of pointing beyond itself, especially through the key Advaita terms *cit* (consciousness), *sākṣin* (the witness or witnessing consciousness) and *jñāna* (knowledge). Each of these terms is given careful discussion in the paper.

With the contribution by Mervyn Sprung, we leave the orthodox (*astika*) schools of Indian philosophy and engage the radical critique of language offered by Mādhyamika Buddhism. In sharp contrast with the Advaita Vedānta view language, here, cannot even point to the reality beyond itself because it is afflicted or diseased (*kleśa*). Language has no revelatory power such as the *vāk* of the Vedas or the *sphoṭa* of the Grammarians. According to the Mādhyamika view, language is simply a conventional creation of man in his ego tainted bondage, and therefore offers no hope of reaching reality. Although they may have a certain practical utility, words, for Mādhyamika, are cognitively worthless. As Sprung puts it, "... all reasoning, based on the everyday understanding of language, must fail to be knowledge, must fail to be anything more than sophisticated screams from the seminars and classrooms of *duḥkha*". Yet even the Mādhyamika must use language, but he does so in such a way, says Sprung, as to use words only which conduce to enlightenment.

In his essay, B.K. Matilal surveys approaches to the ineffable (that which is inexpressible in language) found in the Upaniṣads, Mādhyamika (which he finds to be close to Wittgenstein), Nyāya and the aesthetic theorizing of the Indian Literary Critics. His conclusion is that language can have a function, albeit a most limited one, in relation to the ineffable. He asks the question: can we call something Brahman and again claim it to be ineffable? Matilal's answer is that to respond to the above question in the affirmative involves no logical paradox. "One can say, 'there is something x or some fact which cannot be put into words'. And this statement is not the same as saying 'there is some x about which nothing can *literally* be said'."

Mahesh Mehta takes issue with Matilal's analysis of "the ineffable" as it appears in this paper and in a complementary article "Mysticism and Reality" recently published in the *Journal of Indian Philosophy*. Mehta critically examines Matilal's position point by point and produces what he calls a more positive approach toward the validity of both language and mystical experience. According to Mehta, the varieties of ineffability in linguistic expression should not be taken as antipathy towards language, but rather as devices to nudge one out of complacence at the verbal level and awaken insightful integration with reality.

The final paper, by Leslie Kawamura, differs from the other contributions in that it does not focus on a particular view of language as such. Instead he examines the function of a specific language (i.e. Sanskrit) and its thought forms when used by scholars as a tool for interpreting another religion (i.e. Tibetan Buddhism). As Kawamura demonstrates this results in an imposing of Indian philosophical and psychological systems on an indigenous Tibetan tradition - a practice which has for years glossed over, left unrecognized the uniqueness of Tibetan Buddhism. Yet there is an established view, especially among Sanskrit scholars, that the Tibetan texts are merely the recopying of Indian Sanskrit texts into a new alphabet and grammar. In this view, nothing new is added, and the main value of the Tibetan occurs when the Indian Sanskrit text is lost and the Tibetan text is used to reconstruct the so-called Sanskrit original. Kawamura convincingly argues that such a simple minded view of the relationship between Sanskrit and Tibetan can no longer be held. He also exposes the narrow minded and reductionistic attitude which still prevails when scholars criticize the English translation of an original Tibetan Buddhist text because it does not include Sanskrit terms. In a very real sense Kawamura's essay is living proof of the Mādhayamika view that all language is ego attached, and therefore biased. Is this negative judgement upon language shared by Tibetan Buddhism? Let us all learn Tibetan and find out!

It is a sincere hope of many scholars of Indian philosophy and religion that one day the gap which exists between themselves and their counterparts who specialize in contemporary Western philosophy might be bridged. Most of the above authors have made some initial if often weak move in that direction, by including contemporary Western thinkers in their discussion. As was noted at the outset, the topic of language is current in modern philosophy. Perhaps a curious and open-minded Western philosopher will pick up this volume to see what India does have to say about language. While dialogue with the West would indeed be a welcome result, the main purpose of this volume, and the seminar from which it came, is to foster the critical debate over language in Indian philosophy and religion. It is the hope of the contributors and all those involved in the seminar that the issues raised will help to further our understanding of language within the Indian tradition as well as in other traditions.

The Creative Function of The Word

By KLAUS KLOSTERMAIER

The interpretation of *reality* as *social construction*, mainly through the instrumentality of language and communication, created a minor sensation in Western intellectual circles some ten years ago and is still considered by many sociologists as a break-through in our understanding of the real world in which people live.[1] It may, in fact, connect with a fairly universally held view among the major (ancient) traditions of mankind. After all, is not the true meaning of the original Greek name for poet *maker*? The ancient Greeks considered the *poiḗtes* not primarily a fantasizer or entertainer but a *maker*, a *creator* not so much of tales and fables but of words and worlds.[2] In a quite literal sense does man live in the world made by the poet-creators. Everyone familiar with Indian tradition knows the Devī-Sūkta: the eulogy of Vāc as creator and sustainer of all beings.[3] Similarly everyone familiar with other religious traditions will be able to find parallels to this assumption of the creative role of the word with regard to the beginning and the continued existence of the world: the Hebrew Bible describes the creation of the world as effected by God's word[4] and extolls the role of the *dābār Jahweh* in the course of the world's history;[5] the Greek New Testament associates the existence of the world as well as the salvific enlightenment of mankind with the operation of the lógos;[6] the Winnebago Indians as well as the Maori of New Zealand share this belief in the power of God's word to create the world.[7]

Phenomenologists describe this as a stage in the development of thought when language and reality, word-meaning and thing meant, were considered to be one and the same.[8] In analogy to the creative power of the Supreme Being words spoken by men were thought to possess an efficacy of their own. As A. Daniélou expresses it:[9]

> Speech has the power to evoke images and ideas. The process through which a thought, at first indistinct, gradually becomes definite and exteriorizes itself is similar to the process through which the divine thought becomes the universe. The difference is only one of degree. If our power of thought, our power of expression was greater, things we speak of would actually appear. With our limited powers only their image is evoked. Speech can therefore be represented as the origin of all things. The cosmos is but an expression of an idea,

a manifested utterance. Supreme divinity can be represented as the casual word (*śabdabrahman*).

In contrast to this opinion this essay tries to demonstrate that the endeavours of the human word-makers (as seen in these traditions) are not unsuccessful imitations of the divine world-making, but have a truly *creative* purpose which they are able to really achieve, and that at the core of the ancient traditions with regard to the creative function of the word there is a true and valuable insight into the nature of human speech.

I

A note on the term *creative* may be appropriate at the beginning. In the West *creativity*, *creation*, *create* are terms that have an unqualified positive connotation. In Indian tradition this is not necessarily the case. Comparable terms in Indian languages have a connotation of an order of reality that is derived, secondary, inferior to the realm of the perfect, which is unmovable and inactive. The great creative geniuses of India, men like Gautama the Buddha or Śankara take great care to explain their thought not as *creation* but as a retracing of forgotten eternal truth. They compare their activity to the clearing of an overgrown ancient path in the jungle not to the making of a new path. *Creativity* (in the Western sense) is appreciated insofar as it allows a person to retrace (and reverse) the process of (creative) evolution. The Yogi's creative effort consists in the attempt to undo the evolution of *prakṛti*, to firmly and immovably rest in the first principle and in himself - to be no longer creative! [10]

The *creative function of the word* in our context here consists both in the capacity of the word (*vāk*) to *create* things and to *reveal* their true nature. The two creative functions of the word express thus the basic movements of reality: *pravṛtti* and *nivṛtti*, forthcoming and withdrawal.

These movements do not simply cancel each other out: they propel the evolution of the world and bring it to its completion. They are correlated to each other in such a way as to mutually regulate each other: the *creation* of the world follows a pattern whose fundamental law is the symmetry between *pravṛtti* and *nivṛtti*.[11]

In other words, the understanding of *reality* as *mental* (or social) construct by means of words, although free, cannot be wholly arbitrary, if it is to be meaningful. *Creativity* has a meaning *ab extra*.

Betty Heimann states it thus in the context of the Indian tradition:[12]

> . . . India does make use of the term *fictio* in its positive import. The reality of sense-perception is here never the last and final reality. Like all empirical canons of truth it is of only relative import. True reality lies in the constant transcendental sphere. A visualization and imagination of this highest truth is the utmost achievement to which the Indian thinker can penetrate. As such the *kavi*, the *poet*, is the true *ṛṣi*, *seer* and *saint*. *Fictio*, *imagination*, is the positive mental faculty which forms images beyond the external objects - presentations only of the hidden ideas and ideals which are never fully realizable and verifiable in this world. . . . Pre-existent Matter, true Reality, has more possibilities than those present or of past and future realizations.

Similar thoughts can also be found in the Western heritage. As J. Dalfen in an essay on Plato's dialogues explains:[13]

> It is a Greek assumption that the *logos* as spoken word is an external manifestation of the *logos*, whom we possess as our power of thinking, and that this *logos* is in its own turn connected with, and part of, the *logos* that creates the world and all phenomena and gives them order. This connection is, in Plato's eyes, presupposition for the possibility that the human *logos* can reveal reality in dialogue; but he must follow the *logos* (if he does not do so, and if he says - out of subjective considerations - something other than he thinks *the logos is not right*). This connection is the cause why Plato, when searching for definitions of the *aretaí* constantly brings arguments both from the area of the crafts, the *technai*, and from the area of language: the different areas, structured by the same *logos*, are analogous to each other.

II

Another note may be appropriate on the use of *Word*. From the standpoint of contemporary linguistic philosophy the texts to which I refer use the term in a very loose sense: sometimes it is the equivalent of *name*, sometimes of *meaningful sound*, sometimes of *speech*, and sometimes - in the most crucial instances - it is used for an entity which does not figure in contemporary linguistic analysis at all.[14] It is in the context of the *revealed word* that this entity emerges: a widely shared assumption that knowledge about an ultimate meaning of reality is *given* to (some) men through *revelation* which is concretisized in in sacred scriptures. Now it is a quite common opinion again that *revelation* transcends space and time and cannot, therefore, be identical with a book, or with a multitude of words. *Revelation* consists of *ONE WORD, THE WORD*. *The whole Tora is a single mystical Name* [15] says the Sohar - and it does not even refer to the Tetragrammaton here but to the *Ur-name* which is being revealed time and again to the seeker. It is also noteworthy that the mystical names of God are convergences of optical and acoustical sensations: the Johannine *Logos* is at the same time sound and light,[16] and *nāma* in the Vedic tradition appears both as lightning and as roar.[17]

This amounts to the assumption of a transcendent reality designated *Word* in which all human words partake and which provide their frame and power.

> . . . before the beginning of things, before the manifestation of multiplicity . . . . all *nāmas* were one *nāma*, viz. the unuttered universal *Vāc*.[18]

Creation consists of the (inherent) power of this *Vāc* to become manifold: and *salvation* consists in the (equally inherent) power of man as partaker of *Vāc* to return to this state of oneness. The creative power of the word is made explicit in the identification of Viraj with the hypercosmic *Vāc*.[19] However, according to our texts only *one quarter* of *Vāc* was immolated and turned into the multiplicity of things: three quarters remain in secret.[20] From this one quarter of *Vāc* which is spoken speech, the "higher names were hidden by the *kavis* who watch the seat of *ṛta*" [21] and cannót be perceived by ordinary mortals. Moreover, the one who has been given Vāc in her true nature is silent about her, lest he might lose her by his utterance.[22]

As Marlyla Falk writes:[23]

> Knowledge of *names* is in fact knowledge of things, for according to this ancient Indian conception, the real *nāman* is nowise the fortuitous designation, but the inherent unsensuous essence of the thing to which it belongs.

Nāma thus stands for the inner power of the individual being or thing: the abode of *nāma* is *ākāśa* [24]: *hṛdyākāśa*, the space in the heart, is the domain of *nāma*, the consciousness principle. [25] In post-vedic texts *brahman* replaces Vāc as the designation for the inner power and essence of things. We are all familiar with texts describing the difficulty of attaining to *brahman* - the difficulty to grasp the *Word*.

It may also be important to refer to the widely shared Indian belief that the utterance of a word (especially if it is understood by someone else and its message is fulfilled) takes away its power: the epics know numerous instances of *Ṛṣis* who, in anger uttered a curse which found its fulfillment but which also had the effect of depriving the *ṛṣi* of all his accumulated power. *Creative power* seems to reside in the un-uttered word, the potential utterance - the thoughtfilled silence.

Another synonym for Ṛgvedic *nāma (via ātman* and *brahman)* is finally *satyam.*[26] Knowledge is the reduction of the variety of beings to the primordial unity of being. The power of the Word manifests itself most clearly and specifically in the *sayta-vakya,* the *truth-assertion:* "the *satya* in the truth-assertion is the magical power changing the natural course of things . . . so is the truth of the saving knowledge the power that breaks the fatal course of *samsāra* in leading individual consciousness, by means of illumination, definitely back to its universal source."[27]

In Yogic terminology this was described as a meditative ascension through *śabda* to *aśabda,* the sound as exponent of the soteric aspect of *Vāc* being represented in the *prāṇava*, in OM.[28]

In Vedāntic terminology the *higher brahman* or *vidyā* is at the same time the saving doctrine expressed in verbal form by the divine teacher and the latent divine core of man's being, awakened at the contact of this teaching.[29]

III

Texts from the Indian tradition that deal with the *word* quite frequently analyse not only the finished product but the genesis as well: the production of the sounds that combine into a word. One of the more lengthy texts that does so is the 16th chapter of the Ahirbudhnya Samhitā, one of the major Pāncaratrā Āgamas.[30] Continuing an instruction about the forms of Visnu's Sudarśana or Kriyā Śakti the text tells us that the creative power of Viṣṇu, on which everything depends, is also manifested in the forms of *mantras*.

In the course of the description of this *mantramayī sākṣādviṣṇoḥ kriyāśaktiḥ śuddhasamvinmayī parā*[31] the genesis of the alphabet is explained.

The series of short vowels is related to the sun, the series of long vowels to the moon. The *visarga* is called *sṛṣṭi* (creation), the *anusvāra samhāra* (destruction).[32]

When dealing with the genesis of the consonants we find that this is explained in exactly the reverse order of what we learn on the first pages of our Sanskrit-grammars: both the order of the groups as also the order of the individual consonants within the groups as reversed. In fact we get a mirror-image of the sequence of letters as we know them.[33]

Further we hear that "speech begins with *nāda* resembling the sound of a deep bell"[34] - whereas we know from more popular mystical literature that *nāda* or *anāhat-śabda* is the point where human speech ends, a characteristic of the mystic experience.[35] Symmetry and mirror-images are thus the basic frame in which the word originates and moves.

The same idea seems to be contained in a text from the Tripurā Rahasya, a famous Tantric scripture: it describes the *pratibhā* as the supreme form of the Ultimate Reality and says that on this, as on a mirror the universe is shining like a reflection.[36] The Gorakh-bānis too employ the mirror-simile in connection with the word: [37]

> 24 The *śabda* is the lock, the *śabda* is the key, the *śabda* woke up the *śabda*
> In the *śabda*, through the *śabda*, the experience was obtained and the *śabda* merged into the *śabda*.
>
> 124 Get hold of the *śabda*, O Avadhut! Get hold of the *śabda*!
> The stages (sthāna) are useless obstacles.
> The paramātma becomes manifest within the soul as the moon (is reflected) in water.

Far from decrying the insubstantiality of the *mirror-reflection* the texts seem to emphasise the great worth of it.
As Gorakhāth puts it:[38]

> Neither Veda nor Coran, nor abundance of words: all fell to the bottom.
> At the summit of the sky the *śabda* is shining: there the knower discovers the *alakha* (Invisible Being).

The word that correctly designates a thing is a mirror-reality: as such it has a mediative function. It is on the one hand a real mirror image of a creation not made by man, on the other hand it unifies the scattered (individual) sense-experience (apparent mirror images) into a higher order of being: the real mirror-image. This in turn allows the mind to trace the origin of the mirror-image and unite with the active power that produced it.

It seems that the Indian conception of the world as a word-construct has a good deal in common with the Berger-Luckmann theory. It goes beyond this theory insofar as it assumes the real existence of the cause of the mirror that projects the mirror-image of our world. It is on account of this that the *mental construct* is not *pure fiction* but *realization*. The word, on account of its origin, has reality-content independent of the consensus which it receives in a speech-community. True knowledge, Indian tradition would maintain, does not cease with a knowledge of conventional word-meanings but moves on into the unified cause of all words. From the standpoint of the secular philosopher of language it may be a highly metaphorical use of the term *word* - but the Indian philosopher would maintain that our words are only metaphors of the Word, which contains like a seed all possible words and makes their existence and meaning possible.

For the Brahmanical tradition language itself is of divine origin, the Spirit descending and embodying itself in phenomena assuming various guises and disclosing its real nature to the sensitive soul.[39] The Mīmāṁsakas analysed the problem: What makes a word meaningful? They gave this answer: it is the connection of the word with *ākṛti*, the Uncreated Idea which as such is incomprehensible and never exhausted by the individual word. *Śabda* is in this form ever present and eternal. We do not always perceive it, because its perception depends on its manifestation through the physical word-sound. If it were not eternal the word could not be understood every time it is uttered. The word which we speak and hear is only a partial manifestation of an eternal, meaningful reality; it is not produced by our utterance. Since it is not an effect, it is not perishable either.[40]

The school of Pāṇini, the grammarian, developed this *śabda* philosophy further in the theory of *sphota*. Etymologically *sphoṭa* means a boil which, when opened, ejects its contents all of a sudden. Applied to the problem here it illustrates the fact that the meaning of a word appears all of a sudden after the syllables have been pronounced - none of the individual syllables convey either part or the whole of the meaning. Thus they say:

> The eternal word, called *sphoṭa*, without parts and the cause of the world, is verily Brahman. Thus it has been declared by Bhartṛhari: Brahman without beginning or end is the indestructible essence of speech - it shines forth in the meaning of all things and out of it comes the whole world.[41]

Ultimately, according to this school, all words denote the Supreme Brahman and they maintain that "he who is well-versed in the Word-Brahman attains to the Supreme Brahman".[42]

The *theology of the name* as it is quite common in the *bhakti* traditions emphasises this same thought.

> The Name itself is conceived as unique and as expressing or revealing in a mysterious manner the all-prevading Reality: it is the voiced form of the divine, the supreme *śabdabrahmana*. Rām or Nām is conceived as the supreme *bījamantra*, containing all *truth* or *being (satya)* in itself.[43]

In a very interesting manner this understanding of the *creative function of the word* as the active medium of reality-apprehension ties in with contemporary scientific thought.

The approach to knowledge by way or mirroring and symmetries is becoming increasingly important. Hermann Weyl, whose contributions to mathematics are an integral part of today's calculus has opened up new horizons in his lectures on *Symmetry*, in which he shows the fruitfulness of the symmetry-approach both in nature and art.[44] W. Heisenberg, the great physicist, considered the category of *symmetry* as ultimately only valid and heuristically fruitful one. He pleaded in his later works for a change in concepts in fundamental science, which, he felt was misled by adopting the Democritan idea of atomism. He urged scientists to give up the concept of fundamental elementary particles (which has become somewhat of a metaphor anyhow in the face of more than 100 known *elementary particles)* and to accept fundamental symmetries and related categories as principles in research and physical theory.[45]

The all-pervasiveness of symmetries, and the fruitfulness of the symmetry-approach is again demonstrated in a delightful (but nevertheless serious scientific) work by Joe Rosen: *Symmetry Discovered*.[46] Rosen points out that also analogy is an important kind of symmetry.[47] In science symmetries are closely related to laws of conservation.[48] It will have to be spelled out in detail at a later occasion, how much of the scientists' understanding of symmetries in their own fields can be used to elucidate the nature of speech and language. A cue seems to be provided by K. Lorenz, a Nobel-prize winning biologist in a book which, interestingly, has the (original German) title *The Backside of the Mirror* and is an attempt to contribute to an understanding of human knowledge by way of biology.[49]

Mirror-symmetries are quite fundamental in all life processes: from the beginning of life, when the DNA double-helix divides into two halves, which complement each other by associating free nucleotides to the complete formation of the organism which is largely built on the basis of symmetries. Life processes are to a large extent based on mutuality (Wechselwirkung). In particular he states:

> It is a mistake to divide mind into an external part of speech and an inner part of thinking; in reality both are two sides of one and the same thing. . . . Without doubt the structures of logical thought were given before the development of syntactic language but there is equally no doubt that these structures had not reached their height of differentiation which they have achieved if this mutuality (Wechselwirkung) between thought and speech had not taken place. . . . A child does not really learn to speak, it only learns vocabulary.[50]

Biologists also point out that the specifically human cultural evolution is in close connection with the evolution of that part of the brain which is the center of speech. In a quite literal sense *speech* has created man and his world.

But again, far from inferring from this the total unreality of man's word-world, we have to remember:

> that the apparatus of our cognition is itself a thing of real reality which has received its present shape in confrontation with, and adaptation to, equally real things.[51]

We do not now fall back into the trap of naive realism - but are led to understand our understanding in terms of mirror-image and symmetries to be further explored.

J.C. Pearce in his quite insightful book [52] echoes similar ideas on a more general level when he writes:

> Man's mind is a mirror of a universe that mirrors man's mind, though the mirroring is subtle, random and unfathomable.

In a very precise sense, efforts towards knowledge are efforts towards the word: it is a fallacy to assume (as the LSD theorists did) that a mere shattering of the *reality constructions* (of whose contingencies we are sure!) would reveal *naked and pure reality* as such. All reality is accessible only through the formative activity which culminates in the word.[53] But this word-formation again takes place in a frame: the most creative of poets, musicians, artists, thinkers *discover* rather than *invent* - and if contemporary scientists find that their *discovering* has the character of *inventing* in does not disprove this assumption but goes a long way in stating that all processes of man's creative mind take place in the same frame of mirror-reality and symmetry-finding.[54]

To return to the text of Ahirbudhnya Samhitā, with which we began: According to this, words cannot reveal the nature of Viṣṇu as he is in himself.[55]

> The word may hold the universe within it as its mystic symbol and may represent within it all its energies, but in any case, though it may engulf within it the whole universe and secure the merging of the universe in itself and can identify itself with God, such identification can only be with the Sudarsana power of God, and the entrance into God, or the realization of Him through word or thought can only be through the Sudarsana power, which is a part of Laksmī.[56]

What this seems to mean is that *the center of reality* can only be approached creatively: true understanding can be reached only insofar as someone has reached the creative power and source of words. Only those who have penetrated far enough in their search for the word, to have discovered its mirror-quality (reality) are able to move upwards from the multiplicity of words into the Oneness that gives purpose and meaning that liberates and saves. And only those who have discovered the symmetry underlying this mirrored reality are capable of interpreting *words* in the light of the Word. A dealing with the endproducts as *things* or *facts* will ultimately end in a classification that makes itself redundant, an imitation that fails to stir life, a *saṁsāra* which traps men's minds and condemns them to the prison of the conventions.

CONCLUSIONS:

If we try to sum up the results that seem to be meaningful in our own context: human word-creativity has an essential purpose in the frame-word of the constitution of our world-reality. It seems clear now, that this understanding of the *creative function of the word* was central to the Indian tradition (as well as other tradition), although admittedly a process of *reification* is recognizable in many places where - unawares of the real nature of the creative function of the word - attempts were made to deal with words as if they were material means of production. A renewal of the understanding of the *creative function of the word* would tie in with contemporary attempts to understand the nature of human knowledge as a compound of *creation* and *fact*. Heuristically too, this seems of some importance: the attempt to reach the *śabda-sakti* over and above the *śabda*, *artha* and *pratyaya* [57] would result in creativity and purposefulness of life. True understanding of words requires a foregoing realization, however dim, of the Word as *Śakti*. Only this knowledge of the Word (as source and ground of meaning) allows to relate correctly individual words to each other and go beyond the deal-end factual.

Such a view would avoid both the trap of a metaphysical-monistic reductionism, which totally devalues all human words nor would it allow to narrow the meaning of speech down to the merely technical use of words in dealing with things *qua* things. On the other hand it would lead to a view that encourages men to use language as a creative instrument in relating to reality; a reality neither totally obvious nor totally inaccessible, a reality totally the creation of man and a reality totally given.

It would appear that the frame of *dynamic symmetries* would allow us to unify a variety of otherwise unrelated modes of cognition that are mediated by the word. The word, for one thing, seems to permit also a reversal of time: what is past in the objective-physical sense can be made present in the word and even be projected into the future. Mirror-imaging and symmetries take place in various levels of being that themselves are structured according to symmetries. All this needs time to develop further. At first glance it would seem that also Sankara's understanding of the polarity *māyā-brahman* is based on a fundamental symmetry: proof of this may be seen in the mutuality of superimposition *(adhyāya)*: not only is *māyā* superimposed on *brahman* but *brahman* also on *māyā*! Similarly the Madhyāmika Buddhists with their fundamental assertion: Nirvāṇa is saṁsāra - saṁsāra is nirvāṇa operate with symmetries. It is not a simple identity, nor a simple non-identity but a symmetry that correlates two *realities* that mutually constitute each other.

It needs further thought whether, and how far, symmetry limits and symmetry breaking apply in this context as well.

It is, however, noteworthy that the understanding of the word reality as a mirror-image suggests a visual experience as the basis for *understanding*. Something of this may be behind the Indian custom to have the *darśan* of a saint rather than listen to his teaching (if he chooses to teach at all!) *Symmetry* and *Mirror-image* point towards aesthetic, holistic categories. Quite a few scientists see *beauty* as the last criterium of a finished scientific theory: suggesting the need to *understand* a great variety of details in one glance.

Though this is not the place to go into great detail, it may be permitted to point out that Judaeo-Christian theological tradition could be fruitfully reconsidered in terms of symmetries and mirror-image reality mediated by the creative power of the word. Reflection on man being created in the image of God, on the Word as creator and redeemer, on man being a microcosmos and similar well-known ideas may acquire new actuality in this context.

A reflection on the creative function of the word must end in a consideration of the creative function of silence. Several texts referred to above emphasize the need to move from *śabda* to *aśabda*, from the voiced to the voiceless: in music the pauses are as essential as the notes, in any meaningful conversation the things that are not said are as important as the things said- and it is not mere coincidence that most people need silence in order to deeply reflect and concentrate.

The silence of the Buddha, of Socrates and of Jesus is as meaningful as their recorded words are. The enlightening voiced word is the fruit of the word of silence: the word through which an insight is communicated is later than the insight itself and not really identical with it.

The creative function of word is rooted in the togetherness of sound and silence, of movement and rest, of man's ignorance and knowledge. The word as the medium between man's consciousness and reality as such is the mirror which superimposes the symmetries of man's own thought upon the source of his experiences: to discover finally that man's ultimate name for reality is *Word* - or Silence.

FOOTNOTES

1 P.L. Berger - Th. Luckmann *The Social Construction of Reality* (A Treatise in the Sociology of Knowledge) Doubleday, N.Y., 1966

2 Latin *auctor* (author) meant originally the same; it is a divine attribute!

3 Ṛgveda X, 125

4 Genesis I, 1

5 See Wisdom books and Psalms

6 John I, 3 and 9

7 Mircea Eliade *From Primitives to Zen* Collins 1967 p 83 and 86

8 See S. Morenz, art *Wort* in *RGG* VI, Col 1808 f "Für den Religionsforscher wichtig ist die frühstufige Identität von Wort und Sache, die u.a. in den altorientalishen Hochkulturen gewahrt ist."

9 A Daniélou *Hindu Polytheism* London 1964 p 37

10 According to Patañjali the aim of Yoga is *cittasvṛttinirodha* and *kaivalya,* the condition that is desired is described as: *puruṣārthaśūnyānām guṇānām pratiprasavaḥ* (I,2 and IV, 34)

11 This seems to be the purport of the whole Sāṁkhya system

12 Betty Heimann *Facets of Indian Thought* London 1964, p 174

13 J. Dalfen "Gedanken zur Lektüre Platonischer Dialogue" in: *Zeitschrift für Philosophische Forschung,* April-June 75 (29/2) pp 169-194
Further he states: "Wie der *logos* von Menschen je hervorgebracht wird und ihnen doch vorangeht, so ist auch die *Sache* Philosophie zwar etwas, was sich im Gespräch stets neu ereignet, wozu sich der Mensch je anders stellen kann, die selbst ihm aber als etwas Festes, nicht nach seinem Belieben Abwandelbares entgegentritt . . . (Die) platonisch-sokratische Affassung von der Verbindlichkeit des Philosophierens, von der Notwendigkeit die Konsequenzen des eigenen Denkens anzunehmen, die Konsequenzen des eigenen Denkens anzunehmen, die Konsequenzen des *lógos*, der nach der zu grunde liegenden Uberzeugung immer auch mehr ist als der jeweils eigene . . "

14 Also the Indian philosophers of language apply a more uniform terminology. Individually they distinguish *nāma, śabda, vākya, brahman* quite clearly. I am aware of the risk of trying to develop a kind of general theory of *word.*

15 Sohar III, 36a quoted in G Scholem: Der Name Gottes und die Sprachtheorie der Kabbala, *Eranos* 1970, p 263

16 See note 6

17 See Maryla Falk, *Nama-rupa and Dharma-rupa: Origins and Aspects of an Ancient Indian Conception* Calcutta 1943, p 10

18 Ibid
19 Ṛgveda I, 164, 41 f (X 189 3)
20 Ṛgveda I, 164, 45
21 Ṛgveda X 5, 2 and X 117, 2
22 Ṛgveda X 71, 4f
23 M Falk *op cit* p 16
24 Chāndogya Upaniṣad VIII 14
25 Bṛhadāraṇyaka Upaniṣad II, 3
26 M Falk *op cit* p 24
27 Ibid p 27
28 Ibid p 41
29 Ibid p 49
30 The text has been edited by Pandit M.D. Ramanujacharya under the supervision of F. Otto Schrader and was published in a second revised edition by Pandit V. Krishnamacharya in the Adyar Library 1966 in 2 vols. See also F.O. Schrader *Introduction to the Pāncarātra and the Ahirbudhnya Samhitā* Adyar 1916
31 Ahirbudhnya Samhitā 16 9-10
32 Ibid 73 - 82
33 Ibid 83
34 Ibid 36
35 See R.D. Ranade *Pathway to God in Hindi Literature* Bombay 1959 p 207ff; p 342 *(luminous sound)* 374ff
36 Tripurā Rahasyam (Jnānakhanda) XX 31 ed by Swami Srī Sānatanadevajī: Chowkhamba Sanskrit Series Office 1967 (Kashi Sanskrit Series No. 176) *yatra sarvam jagad idam darpana pratibimbivat*
37 Ch. Vaudeville *Kabīr* O U P 1974 p 137f
38 Ibid
39 T.R.V. Murti *Presidential Address to the 37th Indian Philosophical Congress* p VIII (printed as manuscript)
40 Ganganatha Jha *Pūrva Mīmāṁsā in Its Sources* Benares Hindu University 1942; p 146
41 Madhava *Sarvadarsanasamgraha* XIII 6
42 Ibid XIII 13
43 Ch. Vaudeville *op cit* p 139f
Ibid "The conception of the Satguru as being identical with the all-pervading, supreme Reality, expressing itself not in *voiced* words, even less in written scriptures, but in a mysterious silent *Word* within the hearts of men appears to be central in *Nāthism* whose doctrine Mohan Singh has called *Shabadism* since the *śabda* itself is the true and only key to liberation." (p 139)
44 Hermann Weyl *Symmetry* Princeton University Press 1952

45 W Heisenberg *Tradition in Science* in DIALOGUE 7/1 (1947) p 55 See also his *Physics and Beyond* (Harper 1972) Chapters 19 and 20

46 Joe Rosen *Symmetry Discovered* Concepts and Applications in Nature and Science, Cambridge University Press 1975

47 Ibid p 75 "This is the invariance of a relation or statement under changes of the elements involved in it."

48 A brief introduction in Encyclopedia Britannica (Macropedia) Vol. 5 p 33ff *Conservation Laws and Symmetry*

49 Konrad Lorenz *Die Ruckseite des Spiegels: Versuch einer Naturgeschichte menschlichen Erkennens* Muchen [2] 1973

50 Ibid p 242

51 Ibid p 16f

52 *The Crack in the Cosmic Egg* Challenging Constructs of Mind and Reality, Julian Press Pocket Book 1975 p 85

53 See Ibid p 34

54 H. Weyl *op cit* p 54 "We still share (Kepler's) belief in a mathematical harmony of the universe. It has withstood the test of ever widening experience. But we no longer seek this harmony in static form like the regular solids but in dynamic laws."

55 Ahirbudhnya Ṣamhitā Ch. LI which deals with Lakṣmī as the supreme Sakti of Viṣṇu, into which all other *śaktis* resolve themselves. She is also called the *māyā* of Viṣṇu who is transformed (in part) into the *bhavya* and the *bhavaka śakti*. The *bhavya* shows itself as the world, the *bhavaka* is identical with *sudarśana*.

56 I have adopted Prof. Dasgupta's paraphrase of LI, 69-78 (History of Indian Philosophy Vol III p 52f)

57 Patañjali Yogasūtra III, 17

The Śaiva and the Grammarian Perspectives of Language

By K. SIVARAMAN

The importance of the *word* not only for the idea of revelation but for a variety of ideas forming part of doctrine in Indian thought, i.e., cognition, being, essence, bondage, liberation, etc., is well known. For a proper understanding of the *theological semantics* and the *ontology of the word* characteristic of the generality of Indian tradition, and especially of two of its perspectives taken up for notice in this paper,[1] it is necessary at least, to be critical of some of those features that one has come to accept as too obvious about language to be called into question.

The common assumption at the back of a common-sense understanding of language in terms of words and syllables, and of the more sophisticated approach of structural linguistics in terms of morphemes and phonemes, for example, is the notion that a language is made up of units which are interrelated to form a system, that it is a system of symbols where a *symbol* has meaning by convention, that it is an aggregate of sounds or other concrete phenomena, etc., etc. The true linguistic analogue of *symbols*, of service for performing a complete act of communication all by itself, the sentence-theorist of Indian grammar[2] would say, is not the word, but sentence. One-word sentences exist but they betray their character as not a word by means of their intonation contours. Under what other condition, he would ask, are we justified in saying that a word has two different senses in two different given contexts?

That language is an entity of a more abstract order is, recognised, if not at the common-sensical level, at a more philosophical one (specially of course, where one has no allergy for abstractions). Language even when it is seen to be a system of elements like words and phonemes is recognised to be an organization of abstract elements. Language is an abstraction from particular verbal activities. The latter, i.e., speech, exemplifies and makes possible through its analysis, the discovery of language.

The more popular common-sensical, linguist's perspective and the perspective of the philosopher of language differ significantly over the question of the employment of the term *language*. Language is a system of speech sounds and only derivatively a system of devices for representing them like writing, etc., or alternatively, it is a more abstract non-contingent system of abstract elements of which human speech is only a contingent and not perhaps a very perfect form of embodiment.

From the standpoint of Indian speculations about language, the differing perspectives on this point appear relatively insignificant. Neither of them seem to go a step farther than what is on the surface, i.e., what is but the first of the dimensions or *levels* in the analysis of language. Not even the *philosopher* of language who strives after *ideal* language adequate for philosophical purposes from which structure he hopes to read off basic facts about the metaphysical structure of reality.[3] To understand in a profound sense, the nature of what is, it is necessary to recognise the multi-level or dimensional character of language. The problem of transcending the reality of every-dayness in which we are not in contact with ourselves (symbolising enchainment of existence - *pāśa* in the language of one of the two Indian perspectives about to be considered)[4] is closely bound up with the problem of understanding language in respect of its dimension of depth.[5]

I.

The common basis of the two classical philosophical perspectives on language, viz., those of the Grammarian and the Śaiva thinker is that *word*[6] is the origin of all things inclusive not only of the world of speech but also that of sense or meaning.[7] The notion or origin, it may be noted, imports not causal explanation even though causal category is, indeed, sometimes employed.[8] The *origin* of something, as Heidegger would say in the case of art in relation both to the artist and to the artist's work, is the source of its nature, "that from which something is what it is and as it is".[9]

The idea as a serious philosophical thesis originates from a discussion of the connection between word and meaning, its *apriori*, eternal character affirmed by some and denied by others in the aphoristic and commentary writings of early Indian philosophy.[10] It is not as if the grammarian was primarily concerned with the problems of grammatical nature, of logical syntax, of forms and parts of speech and had no interest in the problem of meaning but became involved with the issue after encountering the classical *darśanās*. According to Paninian system, so we learn from Patañjali, the relation between word and its meaning was held as *eternal*.[11] Earlier still, there is of course the *Vāk Sūkta* of the *Ṛg Veda* wherein Goddess *Vāk* personified as speech describes herself as literally in apposition to everything in the universe.[12] Both the traditions, the Grammarian and the Śaiva, acknowledge the vedic origin of the idea of the word-object isomorphism.[13]

The Grammarian philosophy of language seems to be the precursor for the Śaiva theory, as may be seen from the circumstance that the latter was also later by at least two centuries and also from the reference to the former in the writings of classical Śaiva philosophers by use of descriptive epithets which are indicative of their awareness of it as metaphysically a kindred spirit.[14]

The central thesis of the philosophy of language under discussion summed up in the expression *advaya* or *advaita* is well known: The transcendent word-principle is one; it *manifests* itself (*vivartate*) as many and manifold because of its powers, which is another way of saying that it diversifies itself without at any time ceasing to be one.[15] Consciousness in any form in which it is present to itself is shot through and through with *word*, what is called awareness being never different from the fact of having the form of the word.[16] The unitary word-principle is exemplified as the meaning-bearing unit which is called *sphoṭa*, roughly the semantic counterpart of the syntactical units of word and sentence. Such is then the solution implied in the vexatious problem of the understanding of meaning. What manifests itself as at once word and meaning not only thus encompasses the two constitutive elements of the objective side of experience namely the ontic and the linguistic (*vācya* and *vācaka*), but also encompasses the over-reaching divides of subject and object, i.e., the nominative and the accusative (*kartā* and *karma*) experience and what is experienced (*bhoga* and *bhogya* or *bhoktavya*) and achievement considered as *means* and the same considered as *end*, i.e., the instrumental and the accusative (*sādhana* and *siddha*).[17]

The philosophy of Grammar thus is a classical transcendentalism of the word, accounting for linguistic apprehension in terms of an interplay of two orders or levels of language, that of the individual constituents, the linguistic molecules as it were, and that of a transcendental whole or unity, a form-gestalt operating *unseen* behind the overt and the empirical speech at the audible and the visual levels. The *meaning* is always encountered as a whole, i.e., as a unit, and so must not the generating verbal cognition also be a unit? The speech molecules as individual occurrents in time as such do not generate meaning but they serve to bring into play the unitary word which reveals the meaning unit. The grammar moves within the polar spheres of word and meaning, a philosophy of grammar by means of transcendental reflection seeks for a principle which precedes and thus provides for their polarity, something approximating in its sweep to the religious idea of God, who spans all oppositions as their creator.[18]

II.

Identification of thought and language is typical of Indian philosophy as a whole. Even the empirically and pragmatically inclined of the group, i.e., the *Nyāya Vaiśeṣika* will identify categories of language and the categories of being, defining a *thing* (*padārtha*, literally the word-sense) *inter-alia* as *nameable* (*abhideya*).[19] The *Bhāṭṭa mimāṃsā* thinking also essentially incident to an *exegesis* of the word accords with the general presupposition of the orthodox Indian philosophy of language, viz., the distinction between the meaning-*bearing word* and meaning-*conveying* sound or visual symbol which merely serves to invoke the word.[20] The role of the *sphoṭa* in linguistic apprehension and the implied theory of levels or grades of speech, however, come in for criticism at their hands.[21] Speech functions as one grade only and unless one feels compelled to make the necessary transcendent turn one is not likely to discern distinction of different levels below the surface of speaking.[22]

The Śaiva philosopher too although in many ways closer, and has been, historically, open to the Grammarian doctrine, reacts critically to the *Sphoṭa* theory, not because the theory goes too far or makes a too gratuitous assumption in explaining linguistic cognition but because it does not go far enough. The Śaiva philosopher's penchant for mysticism and in-depth transcendence are reflected in his seeking the core of language in the *silence* of transcendental speech which in turn *waits on* the intuition of God (= Reality). It is not, therefore, surprising that he even questions the propriety of over-stepping the limits of the discipline of Grammar in raising the issue of *saving* knowledge.[23] Instead of truly identifying the liberating insight or intuition the grammarian philosopher could only come up with a counterfeit one deluding himself into believing in its truth. The reference here is to the inevitable self-restriction on the part of the grammarian even when he employs the transcendental method to the level of *paśyanti vāk* precluding him from the still higher reacher of transcendence or, to change the metaphor, preventing him from exploring the deeper layers *way back into the ground*.[24]

Aside from what is signified by this pointed reference to *paśyanti* (to be taken up presently), it is useful to remember that the Saiva critique of the soteriological claims of the Grammatical philosophy of language rests entirely on *apriori* grounds. The Grammarian consistently maintains that the *purification* of the word, a knowledge of the essence of its function is the means to the attainment of the immortal Brahman.[25] Even when it is the case that he is primarily and ultimately engaged in the task of explaining the notions expressed by the forms of Sanskrit Language, and seems as if to endorse that *the limits of his world are but the limits of his language* as when he says that what the word present is alone his *object*,[26] there is no gainsaying of the fact that his interests are those of a *philosopher* in the Indian sense of the term and that his thesis is both a doctrine and an argument.[27] Alternately, the Śaiva philosopher should be the last to ignore the spiritual orientation of the Grammarian especially as he (the Saiva philosopher) accords a place even to the down-to-earch *Cārvāka* materialist in his own scheme of *tattvas* understood expressly as *salvation-horizons* (*mokṣa sthāna*) of every conceivable *spiritual* insight.[28]

What, then, the Saiva philosopher underlines in his critique of the opponent is his own thesis in this connection. The best way of comprehending his own perspective is provided by the archaic-spiritual doctrine of *six-fold Pathway* (*Ṣadadhvan*) barely mentioned or obscurely described in the Tantra literature providing the scriptural basis for Śaivism.[29] The six-fold cosmic-individual pathways comprise of the spheres of word and sense - *varṇa, pada* and *mantra* on one side and *kalā, tattva* and *bhuvana* on the other, and are constitutive of the state of unfreedom (*saṁsāra gati*). Attaining of freedom (*mokṣa*) which consists in the unveiled manifestation of the light of I (*aham*) understood as trans-personal conscious being (*upalabhdrtā prakasa*)[30] involves, precisely, transcending of the *adhvas* (symbolically enacted in the form of the rite of *adhva Śuddhi*).[31] Language in its gross (*varṇa*) transcendent (*pada*) and esoteric (*mantra*) levels operate as an integral part of this six-chambered *nursery* in which the seeds of the fruits of *Sañcita* ripen as it were for harvest. _The answer to the kind of question about liberation that the *vākyapadīa* raises toward the end of its first section, on the Saiva philosopher's own way of understanding things, clearly falls outside the scope of the polar spheres of word and meaning.

Whether the philosopher of grammar was greater than his method of grammar-oriented thinking, influenced as he perhaps was by the Śaivāgama in his insufficiently articulated vision of transcendent work (*parā vāk*), or whether the Śaiva philosopher himself was open to the influence of *Sabda-brahma vāda* formally rejected by him, whatever the truth be the issue between them seems a crucial one.[32] What emerges as the reason of the Śaiva refusal to acclaim the concept of word-principle as representing the ultimate seems to be the relative inadequacy of a merely universal concept of language and meaning and the need for a truly ontological concept which goes beyond the idea of a self-subsistent generic essence, a mere potentiality preceding actualization, a mere locus co-ordinating as equivalents that are different (*Samānādhikaranya*). This is clearly reflected in Somananda's *paśyantī vicāra* in *Śiva Dṛṣti*.[33]

It is to be remembered that while later grammarian philosophers like Nagesa Bhaṭṭa and others enumerate four levels or stages of speech, *Vākyapadīya* itself mentions only three stages[34] that of the one which is unitary, absolutely free from all determination and sequence, beyond all worldly usage, indivisible and imperishable and is the inner light, of the one which is mental (not audible to others) and having sequence *vis-a-vis* the accompanied functions of the bio-motor force called *prāṇa* and, finally, of the one that is overt speech, audible, having definite sequence and form and infinitely diversified. *Sphoṭa*, which is the sentence or word-unit operating *behind* the sensuous syllables and words, is the intermediary one standing between the concrete, manifest kind and the one with the mere impulsion to concretise. The Śaiva critique applies apparently to the *madhyamā vāk* but ultimately to *paśyantī*.[35] An alternate version of the multiple-level theory of language is proposed making emendations on the *paśyantī* side of the spectrum and a consequent reorientation to the sense of these levels from the new perspective that is gained.

III.

Commenting on the etymology of *paśyantī*, the Śaiva philosopher suggests that the root of this transitive verb implies the contemporaneity of its accusative.[36] If the act of *seeing* (*paśyantī*) related to the present were admitted to belong to the highest essence of language or speech, what is the *karma* (accusative) to which it is related? Not the external world because it is only *manifestation* of Śabda so that there cannot be a real relation between the two. *Paśyantī* is allegedly characterized by absence of all duality including that of *kartṛ* and *karma*.[37] It cannot also be maintained that it is related to object through ignorance for then arises the question: is *ignorance* real or unreal? In either case either unitariness will be sacrificed or relation will become false.[38] To admit *paśyantī* itself as unreal will make its interchangeability with brahman meaningless.

It cannot be maintained that *paśyantī* first creates the objects and then sees them. The illogicality of the real creating what is not real apart, it may be asked: are the objects to be created known or unknown to *paśyantī*? To perceive something before creation is impossible while to create the as yet unperceived will offend against grammar.[39]

Paśyantī, to be sure, is regarded as immediately preceding the level of *madhyamā* where temporal order and sequence manifest itself. But then consistently to explain the emergence of sequential order, *paśyantī* should be conceived to be endowed with the latent power of embodying sequence which negates the claim of *paśyantī* to be ranked as ultimate and transcendent. How is *madhyamā* produced from *paśyantī* admitted to be pure being and yet qualitatively (and not merely numerically) different? Neither can it be efficient cause nor instrumental cause as the first will mean dualism and the second substantial identity. If *madhyamā* were identical with *paśyanti*, the latter like the former will be co-eval with illusory knowledge and thus forfeit its claim to be pure knowledge. If, however, it were pure knowledge it cannot manifest plurality of objects but only its own pure nature and *madhyamā* too being identical there with will go the same way, and the external world become *deaf and blind.*[40]

It might be of exegetic interest to note that these earliest interrogations of the doctrine of *Vākyapadīya* involves possible interpretations of it not on lines of the Śaiva theory of Reflection (*ābhāsa vāda*) but on those of the *vivarta* doctrine of *Advaita.*[41] This point is specially striking in view of the greater plausible affinity between *Śabda tattva, kāla Śakti* and *Kalās* in mutual relationship on the one side and *parameśvara, vimarśa* and the different saktis on the other. In both systems of explanation the world is real, in the precise sense in which its reality is questioned by *Advaita*, and the world is *that which is what it is and as it is* having as the source of its nature in the transcendent word.[42] Despite Somananda's acute criticism of *Vākyapadiya* it is perhaps plausible to view the latter as philosophically anticipating the former.

IV.

In fact, indeed, the Śaiva philosopher may even acknowledge his debt to *Vākyapadiya* for quickening his understanding and making it possible to see the need for *parā vāk* from the lead provided by the transcendental analysis undertaken discursively in the text. For what reasons the grammarian holds the *paśyantī* to be the highest aspect of speech, the Śaiva thanks to the grammarian, can see it as but the power of knowledge which in his categorial scheme constitutes the *Sadāśiva tattva.*[43] For him, *parā* as the highest aspect of speech beyond *paśyantī*, is the power of self-awareness or of consciousness being self-aware (*vimarśa*) which is really the point of distinction between sentience and non-sentience.[44] What it meant by *vimarśa* by him is a fusion of the consciousness of self and of the object, the simultaneous knowing of ourselves as knowing something and knowing of that something. It is this aspect of consciousness[45] which makes possible recognition and identification, of the very soul of language, and in this extended sense language is reducible to life itself characterizing animals, birds, fish and the new born baby making it possible to learn, to think, to speak in howsoever small measure.[46]

There is an entire soteriology peculiar to the concept of *parā* in Śaiva philosophy developed in texts like Mahesvarananda's

Mahārtha Mañjari, Abhinava's *Paryanta pañcaśikī* (the opening verse: 'I contemplate on the unspoken speech Para which is the secret, the very nature of the ultimate and which holds within the first, the last and all other powers in between and is the very apotheosis of freedom') and what is perhaps the most important of them, *Parā Trimsika*, a torso of *Rudra yāmaḷa* tantra, with Abhinava's *vivaraṇam*. Abhinava says that the text points to a *third* pathway besides those of knowledge and action, which is called *anuttara*.[47] *Kaulika Siddhi*, as the accomplishment resulting from knowledge of *parā* is called, is explained as what brings about the identity of the sentient and non-sentient just as fire brings about the identity of iron-ball with itself. It consists in the contemplation of *I* (*aham*) a self-identity *preceding* association with body, mind, vital air, etc. The *I* is pure illumination as well as vibrancy (*prakāśa vimarśa maya*) and the entire universe rises from, has its being within, is maintained by and again merges in the same self-identical I. Corresponding to the bi-polar nature of this unity, the universe unfolding out of it is also polarized as word and meaning. The grossest form of *vimarśa* is distinguished from its other forms by association with physical sound. The latter is the manifesting medium having a different physical basis as different from the *ideal* basis in *tattvas* beyond those of *māyā*. Likewise the spoken (*vācya*) ranges between the grossest manifestation of *prakāśa* in the form of *pṛthvi*, etc., characterized by association with *prakriti* and more subtle manifestations in the form of higher *tattvas*, *kalās* and *bhavanas*.

Thus *vācya* and *vācaka* are one in their most subtle original form though in the context of *māyā* they become polarized and become independently variable. This state of perfect unity of consciousness understood in all its diverse modes of action, knowledge and of an incipient motivation (*icchā*) preceding the two, and its contents is what is called *parā* in Śaiva philosophy. The term is used in conformity with the intention to emphasize *vimarśa* side of consciousness in which primordial form language over-reaches all conventions, human, super-human and sub-human alike and makes for their possibility.

The difference between the grammarian and the Śaiva philosopher on the nature of *vāk* held by both alike to be the *origin* of all things, should now be obvious. It is not simply a matter of enumerating more or less. The impression that one may get on a distant pre-view of the Śaiva writing is as if he is saying in effect that to count more is to know more and to know more is to know better. That this is not so, may be seen from the historical circumstance that, though *Vākyapadīya* does not seem to recognise formally at least *parā* as the highest principle in his philosophy, the grammarian thinkers coming after it have accepted it, thus subscribing to the four-fold classification of *vāk*.[48]

V.

The difference, of course, still remains. The difference in the conception of *parā vāk* in the two systems is, briefly, that while in the grammarian's system, *parā vāk* is brahman, for the Śaiva philosopher it is the power of *parama śiva*. True, *parama śiva* and his power known as *vimarśa*, are not different being identical in essence. Yet they stand in the relation of function (*dharma*) and form (*dharmī*). *Dharma* is not a quality or attribute but is the essence of *dharmī*.[49] *Vimarśa* or *parā vāk* is not to be viewed as an independent self-subsistent principle in the same way in which it is conceived in the system of the Grammar school. The Śaiva philosopher is aware of the overlapping of the difference between the extreme position that speech in its essence is reality or being itself (the standpoint of word-absolutism) and the moderate point of view favoured by himself, viz., that speech is essentially not itself *being* but only an actualization of being, part of an inverted dynamism in the structure of being itself. It is the standpoint accepted by the generality of Vedānta both of the absolutistic and the theistic kinds. In soteriological terms, it is the difference between achieving of transcendence *in* language and achieving of transcendence of language itself.

FOOTNOTES

1 The paper purports to focus on one key idea, namely, the parity and disparity of the two notions of *śabda brahman* and *parā vāk*, typical, respectively, of the philosophies of Grammar of Bhartṛhari's *Vākyapadīya* and of Śaivism, primarily of Somānanda's *Śiva Dṛṣṭi*. The paper was originally prepared as part of the proceedings of the Graduate Seminar on Indian Philosophies of Language offered at McMaster's in 1974-75. The writer acknowledges his debt to Drs. J.G. Arapura and P. L. Bhargava and other Graduate students for their friendly criticism and participation.

2 Bhartṛhari refers to the issue between the word-theorist, (*padavādin*), sentence-theorist (*vākyavādin*), one that treats sentence to be such a unit. *Vākyapadīya* III.1.1; Puṇyarāja, II, 20.

3 The use of the mirror analogy in recent western philosophies of language, made current by the early Wittgenstein hinges on the assumption that from the nature of the basic constituents of language one could infer the basic constituents of reality. The generality of Indian speculations on language, the Grammarian and the Śaiva not to speak of the Vedāntin, shows a striking consensus in holding that language could be viewed as a mirror of reality but in a hidden way.

4 See Sivaraman, K. *Śaivism in Philosophical Perspective* Varanasi, Motilal Banarsidass 1972, p. 8.

5 The 'depth-theology of the word' is the aptest description for referring at once to the Grammarian and the Śaiva *philosophies* of language, in contradistinction to the nominalistic, atomistic, conventionalistic philosophies relating to language characteristic of the Buddhistic, the Nyāya-vaiśeṣika and other schools of Indian thought.

6 *Śabda tattva* (word-essence), *śabda brahman* (word-absolute), or simply, *śabda* (word), according to the terminology of the Grammarian, (*Vākyapadīya*, I.1; 116; 120; 123) and *śabdanam* (implicit word) in the technical language of the Kāśhmira Śaiva (*Iśvara Pratyabhijñāvimarśinī*, 1, 2, 1 and 2; 1, 6, 1). In neither of these conceptualizations does *word* depend upon convention (unlike the uttered or manifested kind) and in both it assumes the causal role as internally merged in consciousness or illuminating intelligence preceding, logically speaking, the cognised object.

7 *Śabda prapañca* (word-universe) and *artha prapañca* (meaning-universe), in the picturesque language of the Śaivagama; and, *vācaka* (expressive word) and the *vācya* (expressed meaning), in the linguistically slanted expression of the Grammarian.

8 The causal explanation is invoked as part of the reasoning that the *cause* persists in all its effects and that its

nature can be deduced by observing what persists in all the effects, alike in *Vākyapadīya*, (Vrtti, I, 1, 23) and in the Śaivāgama which also employs the language of *jñāpaka hetu* (*causa cognoscendi*) in this connection. For use of *hetu* to comprehend the sense of *jñāpaka* see *Vākyapadīya*, III, 7.4. Commentary which admits parallel running of the cosmic process. Śaṁkara admits the thesis of the word-origin of things as Scriptural (*Bṛhadāraṇyaka*, I.2.4.; *Taittirīya Brāhmaṇa* II, 224, 2), but controverts the implication of word being the *Causa Materialis* of things, *Brahma Sūtra*, I.111.28. Commentary.

9 Heidegger, M. *Poetry, Language, Thought* New York Harper & Row 1972 p 17. *Apropos* what Heidegger says about the artist and his work of art, it can be said about consciousness and content that 'in themselves and in their interrelations they *are* each of them by virtue of a third thing, which is prior to both, namely that which gives them their names' - *śabda* (keeping in mind the respective description of consciousness and its content as *śabdopagrāhi* and *sabdopagrāhya* by the Vṛttikāra, *Vākyapadīya*, I, 123).

10 *Mīmāṃsāsūtra*, I, i, 6 to I, ii, 17 Nyāya Sūtra Book II Chapter II 59 to 69 *Brahma Sūtra* I.III, 28

11 *siddhe śabdārtha sambandhe*, *Mahābhāṣya*, I.1.1. Patañjali discusses the cited *vārttika*, interprets types of eternality imported by the expression *siddha* and makes a statement which has become classical: 'What does it matter to us (Grammarians) to know what is eternal and what is not eternal?' For Bhartṛhari's comment on this statement as expressive of a positive intention of the philosophy of grammar to accommodate itself to all the *darśanas*, vide, Subramania Iyer, *Bhartṛhari* Poona 1969 p 74

12 *Ṛg Veda* X, 125, rk 8

13 *Vākyapadīya* I, 120; *Śiva Dṛṣṭi* III, 66 Commentary

14 *vaiyākaraṇa śabdādvaita*, *śabda parabrahmādvaita*, etc. *Śiva Dṛṣṭi*, III, 1. opening remarks of the Commentary

15 *śabda tattva brāhmaṇi ekātvavirodhinyaḥ samucitaḥ ātmabhūtaḥ śaktāyah śānti*, etc. *Vākya* I.I.2. Commentary

16 *Vākya*, I, 115. This is also the view of the Śaiva though expressed in a different terminology: *pratyavamarsa*, as the essence of *citi*, which is the transcendent word (*parā vāk*). See *Iśvarapratyabhijñāvimarśini*, I, 5, 11, 13

17 Iyer op cit p 147

18 *yo hi paśyati paśyanti sa devaḥ paramo mataḥ*, *Śiva Dṛṣṭi* 3, 63-64

19 Kuppuswami Sastri *A Primer of Indian Logic* Madras 1932 p 5

20 Murti, T.R.V. *Some Thoughts on the Indian Philosophy of Lan-*

guage Presidential address to the 37th session of the Indian Philosophical Congress 1963

21 Kumarila's *Tantravārttika* Ānandāśrama edition p 293ff

22 *avibhāge tathā śaiva kāryatvena avatiṣṭhate*, *Vākya*, I, 1, 127

23 *vaiyakaranatam tyaktva vijñānabhaṣaṇena kim ? Śiva Dṛṣṭi*, III, 72-73

24 Heidegger, M. *The Way Back into the Ground of Metaphysics* in Kaufman, W. *Existentialism* New York Meridian Books 1956 pp 208ff

25 *tad vyākaranam āgamya para brahmadhigamyate*, *Vākya*, II, 22

26 *arthaśca asmākam yah śabdena abhidhīyate*, *Mahābhāṣya*, I.1.1. see ante note 11

27 *darśana, vāda;* see Iyer op cit Chapter 3 *Bhartṛhari and the darśanas*

28 Sivaraman, K. op cit p 55ff

29 *Svacchanda Tantra*, II, 50, *Mṛgendra Tantra*, adhvaprakaraṇa, *Paryanta Pañcāsika* sloka 4 Sivaraman op cit p 383-405

30 *Iśvarapratyabhijñavimarśini*, I, 1, 1

31 Sivaraman, K. *op cit* p 385

32 For a detailed discussion, see, Gaurinath Sastri *Philosophy of Word and Meaning* Calcutta Sanskrit College Research Series no. 5 1959 pp 66ff

33 *Śiva Dṛṣṭi* chapter III

34 *Vākya*, I, 134

35 *Śiva Dṛṣṭi*, III, 58-61 for refutation of *sphoṭa*, III, 40 for refutation of *madhyamā* and the entire chapter for refutation of *paśyanti*

36 *vartamana samaruddha kriyā paśyantyudahrta dṛṣih sakarmako dhātu kim paśyanti iti kathyatam* ? ibid III, 20

37 ibid III, 33

38 ibid III, 34

39 ibid III, 35, 36

40 ibid III, 40 *andha mukham jagad bāhya sarvameva bhaviṣyati*

41 Gaurinath Sastri op cit p 61

42 Cf with the Advaitin's sense of non-difference, e.g. Śaṁkara's commentary on *tadanyatvam arambhana śabdadibhyah Brahma Sūtra*, II, 1, 15

43 *artha asmakam jñanaśakti ya sadaśivą rupini vaiyākarana sadhunām paśyanti sa parā sthitih*, *Śiva Dṛṣṭi*, III, 26

44 *Iśvarapratyabhijñā Kārikā*, I, 5, 11

45 Described variously as *citi*, *pratyavamarsa*, *ahampratyavamarsa abhilāpa*, *śabdanām parāvāk*, Kṣemarāja's *Parāpraveśika* p 2 see Iyer op cit p 107

46 See *Nādakārikā* 15 commentary for a parallel notion of *nāda* Sivaraman op cit p 548-549

47 For a concise analysis of the notion of *anuttara* developed in

the light of its rich polyphany by the text, see Pande, K. *Abhinavagupta* second edition Varanasi 1963 p 635ff

48 ibid p 625

49 For a discussion of the distinction of Śakti and Śiva in terms of *dharma* and *dharmī*, see Sivaraman op cit p 519

Reflections on Some Key Terms in Advaita Vedānta

By DEBABRATA SINHA

I.

In our discourse on the philosophy of language implicit in the system of Advaita Vedānta, we propose to start with a preliminary skepsis regarding metaphysical language as such. Rational metaphysics, that is an intellectualistically constructed system of metaphysics, seems to present a fundamental puzzlement in respect of language. It is the extension of natural factual language -- quite often in a naive overdefinite manner -- for representing truths acclaimed to be of *higher order*. This whole claim of putting up a presumably different set of language, which is natural in form and appearance and yet non-natural (or over-natural) in import, has, with ample justification, invited radical criticism from the sceptic and the positivist in modern philosophy. We are at least alerted by the deeply sceptical note posed by Nietzsche: "Is language the adequate expression of all realities?" How far can the language conventions be treated as "really the products of knowledge, of the sense of truth"?[1]

It may be worthwhile to try a fresh look at the so-called higher order truths in a way other than that of a strictly formal-deductive system of statements derived from certain concepts and principles taken as postulatory axiomatic truths. There may be a possible alternative way of constructing a language system -- and in a way, a system of metaphysics is a system of language. Instead of an *a priori*-conceptual analysis, a reflective (transcendental) critique of experience might proceed by way of analysing essence-implicates of the given in experience at various levels and degrees of reflection. This can broadly be characterized as the *phenomenological* approach (not necessarily in the strict sense of Husserlian Phenomenology) in the interpretation of experience in its depth, bringing about a corresponding mode of expressions or language.

II.

Coming now to the classical system of Advaita Vedānta, it seems to present the paradigm of a metaphysic of experience which could be read in broadly phenomenological terms. No doubt Vedānta has the formal appearance of a metaphysics (maybe, even theological metaphysics) -- a rationally organized system of explanations regarding such fundamental issues as Man, World and God. Yet it can hardly be taken simply as an intellectualistic metaphysics, with its set of rationally constructed expressions which would refer *a priori* to the structure of Reality.

There is one basic note of predicament running through Vedānta thought -- right from its origin in the Upanishads. How to meaningfully communicate through language that supposed core of intuitive insight or experience which, from the very nature of the case, cannot be translated adequately in natural language, nor fixed in terms of well-defined concepts and categories? Such translation could be possible only through undermining the very living integrity of concrete experience itself. The Upanishads refer to the ultimate principle (*Brahman* or *Ātman*) as 'that from which words turn back, along with mind, not having attained'.[2]

For an avowedly intellectualistic system of rational metaphysics such a predicament would not be so pertinent. There may, however, be another way -- perhaps more direct, if not simplistic one. That is the way of *mysticism* outright -- that is, viewing the supposed contents of spiritual intuition altogether as intellectually baffling and totally impervious to common knowledge and experience. Such an approach, again, would miss the whole thrust in Advaita thought of addressing itself to standard human experience and reason, and to work its way through in-depth interpretation of experience up to the essence *par excellence*. The Upanishadic characterization (negative) of the Real as beyond the grasp of speech and mind (*avākmānasagocaram*) need not mean an easy and premature surrender of our faculty of understanding.

Advaita philosophy does no doubt take its cue from the negative mystical statements of the Upanishads concerning the completely ineffable character of Brahman, the end point of the quest. It is acknowledged that the Absolute cannot be spoken of literally; but that does not prevent the Vedāntist to contend that words can still indicate the presence of Brahman in an indirect way -- not *vācyārtha*, what is meant through word or as spoken of, but *lakṣyārtha*, what is indirectly indicated. Thus the thrust of Vedāntic concepts and expressions is not to refer to fixed objects or objective facts, and as such in no way ostensively definable. Their meaningfulness is not to be confined to the objective referent within the world of natural experience; negative language (*neti neti*, etc.) would be more pertinent in that context.

So what is operative in the Vedāntic analysis of language is not the *semiotic* attitude that words serve as vehicle for concepts, which again are names for sensible objects. Advaita would not as such be averse to natural or object language; but it is too keenly aware of the limitations of such language in describing the *transcendental* situation. In that sense it does present reflection on natural language -- but not *qua* language. Thus it does not propose any formalistic investigation into the syntactical-semantic structure of language, nor does it offer, strictly speaking, a system of *meta-language* (unless the latter is taken broadly in the sense of a reflective second-order language).

The Advaita attitude to language would basically depart from the common presupposition in the Western tradition of drawing a strict dichotomy between language and extra-linguistic reality. Whether in classical Western thought, Socrates and Aristotle, or in recent thinking of Russell and Wittgenstein or Quine and Chomsky -- the philosopher of language, in some way or other, has been intrigued by the problem of bridging the gulf between language and reality. The one way which has been suggested (both in Aristotle and in early Wittgenstein -- though in entirely different contexts) is some sort of an *inferential* step. Even the Indian school of Nyāya-Vaiśeṣika seems to follow the way of inference in their passage from the analysis of empirical notions to the categories (*padārtha*) of reality.[3]

The Advaita philosophy of language (if we can speak of one as such) does not in the same way look for fixed reality *behind* language. In this respect Advaita would rather join hands with Mīmāṃsā. As in the latter, in the Vedāntic context the words (*śabda*) have autonomous function of their own, not limited to the function of serving as means of expression for concepts to be communicated in complete and precise terms. For the Mīmāṃsā philosophy, there is intrinsic relation between the indicating words (*vācaka*) and the object indicated or meant (*vācya*). But while for Mimāṃsā the autonomous function of language operates entirely in the prescriptive context of ritual practice, for Advaita, proceeding entirely in the context of cognitive reflection, terms *symbolically* convey the ideal possibility of perfected intuition. This *symbolic* use of language will be subsequently explained. Accordingly, the issue of knowledge through verbal testimony (*śabda-janya-jñāna*) takes on a very special role in the Vedāntic scheme. The words of the scriptural texts concerned -- or rather the major statements of *Śruti* (*mahāvākya*, as they are called) -- are accepted as having a deeper suggestive function rather than used for ostensive definition or description of a fact or an objective situation.

Along with the essential recognition of this deepr suggestive function of language, Advaita is at the same time keenly aware of a possible misleading function of language too. Thus a word may be taken as the adequate expression of a concept, but on reflective probing, may turn out not to be so at all; or its meaning may conceal something which leads the investigator in the wrong direction. This caution on the misleading role of language in prematurely and over-definitively fixing the nature of higher reality in terms of familiar words and concepts is there right from the Upanishadic negative statements like *neti neti*.

This negative slant in respect of our language and thought habits determines the Advaitic mode of definition of the Absolute as in the standard formulation in terms of *Sat-Cit-Ānanda*. By way of double negation the Absolute is referred to as the negation of all that is *asat* (non-being), *acit* (non-consciousness) and *anānanda* (non-bliss). There is no question of these three double negations to be either identical with, or different from, one another. The absolute has just to be understood as the negation of the world which is demonstrated as non-*sat*, non-*cit* and non-*ānanda*. As for the relation between this negative *non-world* and the positive absolute, the two are non-different, only spoken of in two different ways in the empirically conditioned (*vyāvahārika*) mode of speech.

III.

In order to grasp the so-called *symbolic* use of language in Advaita discipline, we have first to concentrate on the central concept which forms the pivot in the Advaita metaphysic of experience, viz., *Cit* (or *Caitanya*). An apparent puzzlement might show itself in the Vedāntic understanding of *Cit*, which means consciousness and yet indicates, in terms of Vedāntic definition itself, what is ontologically trans-individual as well as overmental. The question is: Can we meaningfully speak of consciousness, without confining it to the psychological realm of being and to the frame of reference of the individual (*jīva*)? But that is what *cit* presumably indicates, when spoken of as the very essence of self or *ātman*.

Phenomenologically viewed -- that is, viewed on neutralizing the natural attitude, or exercising what Husserl would call *epoché* or *bracketing* of the factual-existential positing -- *cit* has to be translated as *transcendental subjectivity*. It does not indicate even the mental-psychological fact, but something over-mental over-natural. Even the psychological state, for Vedānta, pertains to the level of the objectively presentable -- that which can at least be object of psychological introspection. But *cit* is unambiguously characterized (negatively) as *unobjective* (*aviṣaya*).

This negative moment of unobjectivity -- or *uncognisability*, as later Advaita puts it -- marks the point of departure for the genuine attitude in the understanding of *cit* as pure consciousness. The whole point about this negative moment in the definition of consciousness -- that it is in principle incapable of being an *object* of possible cognition, as any other thing or being -- is to emphasize that this pure essence of consciousness is not to be understood in an entitative fact language. Not only is *cit* to be understood as non-physical non-physiological, but also as non-mental.

Yet *cit* is not posited as an abstraction, but is supposed to be there essentially involved in the complex of bodily, vital and mental existence that is tied up with the living empirical individual (*jīva*). The way of Vedāntic reflection is to dissociate the possible pure essence (or essences) from all the contextual conditions in which it is functionally immanent. Consequently, the steps of withdrawal from the associational conditions (*upādhi*) through steps of gradual progressive (or, viewed from the other end, regressive) reflection. *Cit* is thus a word which does not so much represent a fact which is fixed and realized, but rather conveys a constant continuous *demand* in reflection for the highest possible essence. The latter stands out as unconditionally autonomous -- free from even the last vestige of individuality and mentality.

Advaita, however, has an emphatic positive language in respect of *cit*. In a pseudo-metaphorical expression it is defined as *svaprakāśa*, that is, self-illuminating or self-manifest, inheriting directly from the Upanishads their favourite image of light and the sun. Transcendental reflection here is supposed to end with the highest essence, that is *cit*, as revealing or unfolding itself in all its pristine purity and autonomy. The typical definition in terms of *svaprakāśatva* seeks to combine the limitations of object language (which also incorporates the description of the mental states and events in psychological terms) along with the positive accent on self-evidencing immediacy. It implies a turn to a dimension other than the objective-factual. Advaita would not have any slightest reservation that *cit* is real unlike pure consciousness, described as "phenomenological residuum", in Husserlian phenomenology. Only it is real in a way quite different from what conceptual definition of objective reality could state.[4]

Looked at from the perspective of a possible *cit*-centric critique of experience, as briefly indicated above, one significant feature in the Advaitic treatment of language is apt to emerge. As already pointed out, one can speak of a *symbolic* use of language in the Vedāntic description of the essence-wise (not natural-objective, nor formal-apriori) structure of experience. In that context of transcendental reflection essentialities are sought to be drawn out from within the experience-continuum at various levels of givenness. In and through the region of purified (in the phenomenological sense, what is to be gained through *reduction*) experience, *cit* emerges as *the* essence.

Now, while *cit* by very definition is not amenable to objectification, it is still recognized as somehow capable of being *symbolized* -- that is, represented indirectly. In the gradual dissociation of transcendental consciousness from the mental states (*vṛtti*), in which the former is found to be functionally involved, the mental states or stadia which are transcended are sought to be understood as functions (or functional correlates) of the content, or complex of contents, by way of translating, in a forward-looking language, the essentialities which present themselves in the process of withdrawing from the associated manifolds. That is why such language as of Advaita, with its terms and categories, can be called *symbolic* -- conveying the indepth possibilities of the transcendental order rather than portraying the realities of the empirical or of the metaphysical order. Thus symbolic concept-formations come to work on the various levels of external physical and bodily-mental phenomena.[5] In this respect, it is no doubt true, in later Advaita the terms are often used in a formalized fashion of a stereotyped metaphysics, shifting more or less from the phenomenological foundations in evidence-intuition.

IV.

The close-knit cluster of selected concepts, which centre around the notion of *Cit* in framing out the Vedāntic analysis of experience, come up for consideration in our present discourse. The foremost among such concepts is *Sākṣin* (or *Sākṣi-caitanya*), which literally means *witness* or *witnessing consciousness*. The status of self or consciousness -- the Advaita conception of self (*atman*), on ultimate analysis, being absolutely equivalent to pure consciousness (*cit*) -- is modelled on the role of an observer in common life, or may be a law-court witness. What is meant is the transcendental function of consciousness in respect of the manifold of mental states and experience. To put it in another way, *sākṣin* indicates the moment of free reference or evidencing on the part of consciousness. As the typical definition in Vedānta puts it, *sākṣin* implies only *seeing*, that is evidencing, without any agency or *doing* being involved therein (*akartṛtve sati draṣṭṛtvam*). The burden of the concept is thus concentrated on the transcendental-functional moment of consciousness, with its possibility of standing apart from the complex of mental states, and yet *freely* referring to them.

Viewed phenomenologically, *sākṣin* need not be fixed as the concept denoting either a factual situation or a soul in the common metaphysical sense, but rather as signifying the possibility of pure consciousness in its transcendental role. Admittedly, there seems to be some apparent ambiguity about defining the ontological status of *sākṣin* in the long run, so far as Vedānta goes beyond the *sākṣin* stage -- in fact, beyond the dichotomy of the evidencer and the evidenced. However, it certainly marks the apex in what may be called a *phenomenological hermeneutic* of *Cit*.

In this context an analysis of the related term, *ahaṃkāra*, is called for. It is the commonly accepted word in Sankhya and Vedānta systems, indicating ego or egoity -- in other words, the I-principle. No ego-substance, however, is to be posited outright, as referred to by the notion of *I*. In fact Advaita would not formally recognize the ontological validity of *ahaṃkāra*, although it bears an ontic significance in the vedāntic scheme of analysis of experience. I-notion or ego-sense is an undeniable element in human consciousness, although in a way notoriously elusive. To trace the true essence (not pseudo-essence) of what is denoted by *I* would pose a puzzlement not only for the neo-behaviourist analyst, (like Ryle), who would explain it away in terms of *systematic elusiveness*, but in a deeper way for such transcendentalists as would not be ready for a premature commitment of Cartesian *ego cogito*. And Vedānta does not yield to the lure of such ego-substance, conforming directly to the I-notion.

On the other hand, Vedānta is quite emphatic on the point that I-consciousness combines in a uniquely intriguing manner the two apparently contrary elements of *this* and *not-this* -- *idam-anidam-rūpa*. In other words, it partakes of the characters of what is presentable as object and what is never capable of being so presented and designated. It marks the nodal point of fusion (*tādātmya* or false identification) between consciousness and the natural-factual, where-from, as Śankara points out, the whole series of natural-psychological co-efficients of subjectivity follow -- agency, enjoyership, cognisership, etc., all necessarily intelligible in the context of objective world. The point is directly made when it is said that *ahaṃkāra* is the *knot* binding together consciousness and the non-consciousness -- *cit-acit-granthi* -- indeed the hardest knot for the reflecting subject to unravel.

One question which would arise at this stage is: does not Śankara himself (in his introduction in *Brahma-Sūtra-Bhāṣya*) prima facie define the subject (*viṣayī*) as that which is amenable to the notion of *I*? If the level of egoity admittedly belongs to the sphere of spiritual confusion (that is, *adhyāsa*), how could the highest essence again be referred to as *I*? In spite of the Vedāntic denial of mind and egoity to the claim of *Cit*, there still seems to remain some room, though not in an explicit manner, for positing *pure I*. In fact it would not be illegitimate to designate *sākṣin* -- or also the other related term, viz., *Pratyagātman*, which means innermost self -- somehow as *pure I*.[6] In designating transcendental consciousness as *I* (though as *pure*), there is involved some kind of *an essential equivocation* -- as Husserl acknowledges it in the context of the phenomenological problematic of the relation between ego and *transcendental I*.[7]

Vedānta is indeed cautious not to mix up *cit* or *ātman* with a hypothetical I-substance, the I-notion hypostatised into a metaphysical concept, as the ontology of Nyāya-Vaishesika, for example would do. The whole nexus in Vedāntic reflection lies in the direction of over-individual reality -- and the departure from, or transcendence of, individuation comes into play at the highest point of inwardization in individual consciousness.

V.

One term which is so uniquely characteristic of the Vedāntic standpoint, but is yet so general in its import, is *jñāna*. *Knowledge* which is its obvious translation, is rather a blanket term that can conceal within itself ambiguity. The whole drive in Vedantic thought and culture is said to be *jñāna*; knowledge of self is said to be the only way of attaining the highest freedom (*mokṣa*). It is primarily the way of knowing, and only secondarily of willing (*karma*) and feeling (*bhakti*). But the question is: if it is the ideal of cognitive freedom, how is this *jñāna* related to cognition in the ordinary sense of the word *to know*? Here the usual epistemological model of knowledge-of-object (through some medium direct or indirect) is apt to come into play and thwart our understanding of the meta-epistemic model that Vedānta originally adopts from the Upanishads. In characterizing *ātman* or *cit* -- or for that matter, *mokṣa* itself -- as *jñāna*, what is intended is direct evidencing (or *seeing*) that inevitably turns into the very immediacy of being. Śankara emphatically urges the point when he speaks of this ideal of perfect knowledge (*samyak jñāna*) as nothing but getting at the complete intuitive comprehension (*avagati*).

Jñāna, it is true, came to be treated predominantly in the epistemological context. A distinction of levels has, of course, been drawn between the mental mode (*vṛtti*), or modalisations of the internal organ (*antaḥkarana*) in the form of objects, on the one hand, and pure consciousness as the transcendental element, on the other. While the former implies the moment of object-reference, the latter indicates the ideal moment of transcendental subjectivity. As one later Advaita thinker points out[8], the word *jñāna* is used in three different senses: (a) the primary pre-epistemic level of bare *vṛtti* -- it can be termed *jñāna* rather abstractly, indicating the unreflective use of object, not amounting to cognition proper ; (b) only with *vṛtti* qua psychic state, that is as conscious (in relation to evidencing consciousness), we have cognition of object; (c) but Advaita proceeds further to the transcendental level of pure evidencing behind all particular modalisations in this or that form of object, external or internal (mental).

Jñāna in the third sense is equivalent to *sākṣi-caitanya*. But even at this point, which can otherwise be regarded as the terminal of phenomenological reflexion, Advaita would finally tend to move beyond the detached consciousness of a spectator, to whom all objectivity is presented. Such *knowledge* no longer would conform to the strict cognitive model, but is rather to be understood in the original Upanishadic sense of enlightenment that is nothing but spiritual being. The latter would admit of no differentiation between the subject reflecting and the content reflected upon. That would imply the transcendence of the phenomenological (and to that extent, epistemological) modus operandi proper.

In later Vedānta, it is true, we find a rather too easy equivalence between the two models of knowledge -- namely, *jñāna* as the immediacy of intuition (*aparokṣa-anubhuti*) and *jñāna* as *pramāṇa*, that is strict cognition through ways of knowing. The former is even sought to be interpreted sometimes on the model of the latter more or less. However, the unmistakable accent on *jñāna* in Śankara brings out the contemplative attitude of the Upanishads, focused on the intuited essence in spiritual reflection, undeterred by subjective psychological factors and conditions. This is what Śankara means when he speaks of knowledge being entirely determined by *the thing* (*vastutantra*) rather than by any *personal* process (*puruṣa-vyāpāra-tantra*).

The paradigm statement of the Upanishad (Muṇḍaka Upanishad) that *knowing Brahman one becomes Brahman itself*[9] cannot be taken intellectualistically, but rather in the light of that ideal model of integral experience wherein the contemplating subject would lose itself in the self-revelation of truth. The over-all knowledge slant in Vedānta brings into focus the fundamental truism that spiritual being, the culmination of the *Mokṣa* drive, has the self-illuminating character as that of knowledge, whether implicitly or explicitly, unrealized or realized.

FOOTNOTES

1 F. Nietzsche "On Truth and Lie in an Extra-moral Sense" in *The Portable Nietzsche* ed. W. Kaufmann, Viking Press, New York, p. 45.

2 Cf. "Yato vācāh nirvartante aprāpya manasā saha ..." *Taittiriva Upaniṣad* II.9.

3 In this context one may cite relevantly the general attitude of the so-called *linguistic phenomenology* (of Austin), which generally seeks to obliterate the dichotomy between language and fact.

4 Nor is the characterization as subjective reality appropriate in respect of *Cit*; for even pure *subjectivity* would not be the right definition of its ultimate ontological status (as de-individualized).

5 Here the expression *symbolic* is used not in the sense of any religious symbolism as such. What is meant in this context is the raison d'etre of a symbolic situation: not the knowledge of being (the highest Being, as the case may be) qua being, but suggesting the ontic possibility of higher essence (or essences) beyond what could directly be meant or referred to by a term (as real being).

6 Cf. Husserl speaks of *pure I*, *transcendental I*, *transcendental ego*, etc. -- all as equivalent expressions, without meaning any definite metaphysical principle of self or soul.

7 Edmund Husserl *The Crisis of European Sciences and Transcendental Phenomenology*, p. 184.

8 Sarvajñātma-muni, *Saṁkṣepa-Śārīraka*.

9 Cf. "Brahma veda brahmaiva bhavati" *Muṇḍaka Upaniṣad* III.ii.9.

Non-Cognitive Language in Mādhyamika Buddhism

By MERVYN SPRUNG

This paper wants to lock horns with a central question in the philosophy of Mādhyamika Buddhism: how natural language can serve the purposes of enlightenment. It is perhaps foolish to attempt this as no one has yet locked horns with Mādhyamika who has not been thrown -- and lost his horns in the struggle. The question deals with a philosophy of language but concerns the human predicament, the concern of all classical philosophies. How extricate the human from his natural predicament without mutilating his greatest gifts? Courageous bondage may be more enlightened than passive liberation. To discuss any question in Mādhyamika apart from this central concern would be I believe, to distort it, and the question of language is no exception. Nāgārjuna, Āryadeva, Candrakīrti and the others do not develop an explicit philosophy of language but we should be able to learn a great deal if we study what they say about language. If we do not isolate this from the central concern of their thought, it should light up some approaches to Mādhyamika understanding of the human predicament and its transcendence.

THE NATURAL PREDICAMENT

The buddhist, of whatever school, has so much in common with what might be called a naturalist and what is most often called a nihilist that he is at pains to defend himself against the charge of being one. He turns naturally to the phenomena, inner and outer, mostly the former, of everyday existence and tests their behaviour by his own experience. He is without obtrusive presuppositions and cool in his analysis. He is quite fearless in drawing his conclusions about the meaninglessness of the natural order and the virtually hopeless predicament of all beings, including the human, who are seemingly inextricably interwoven with it.

The Mādhyamika understanding of the human being begins with a spontaneous conscious event (*ayoniṣo manaskāraḥ*) (*Prasannapadā*, p. 452). This is not a *state*, nor an *act*, it is an unaccountable psychic spontaneity below the level of all other acts and faculties. It is dynamic, volative, action-bent, generating and carrying all differentiated human activities. This underived beginning is understood as a thirst or hunger (*taṇhā*) for not less than everything, but, in that sense, for inexhaustible existence itself. This is perhaps an attempt to describe the nature of the psyche itself, an attempt recalling Freud, Nietzsche and Schopenhauer.

The most primary set of acts resting on *taṇhā* consists of the judgments *good* and *not good* and fixing a world of putative things based on these (*śubhāśubhaviparyāsa*). In a world with this skeleton structure it is possible for the *kleśas* to arise. These are the basic afflictions of beings, the express finitude of natural existence, the limitations within which beings must decide and act. They may be many -- any form of helplessness due to preformed value judgments -- but the Mādhyamika texts speak, classically, of three: *rāga, dveṣa* and *moha*, or 1) being attracted to what is considered *good*; 2) being averse to what is considered *not good*; and 3) being deluded by the putative substantiality of the good and not good things. The *kleśas* dictate the basic forms of involvement in the world. Specific actions of responsible individuals arise within these limitations and, of course, from action consequences must arise as *fruition*, to use the buddhist term. Fruition may require many birth-death episodes because of inexorable *karma*.

In this way beings are driven, by the nature of existence itself to perpetuate their hopeless strivings and ambitions meaninglessly. No aspect of natural human existence escapes this condemnation. There is no value sense nor faculty of reason which is of another origin and not an integral part of kleshnic finitude. Reason, especially, or more strictly, intellect, is as much in the service of the pervasive hunger for existence as are passions and ambitions. The intellect is an expression of this hunger. In the natural man, strictly as such, there is no divine spark, neither in the form of a universal reason (Aristotle) nor of a transcendent love of the good (Plato), nor of immanent *brahman* (Vedānta).

LANGUAGE IN ITS NATURAL SETTING

This view of the natural predicament of humans obviously severely restricts the possible views of the nature of human language. There is nothing in man's nature which could infuse meaning, other than empirically generated meaning, into human language. There is no Upanishadic immanent *brahman*, no platonic memory of the forms of Being nor any Christian God-created soul. Language must be as afflicted, as diseased as all other elements on the natural scene. It can hardly be used to uncover truth. It has no revelatory power. *Vāc* is not the most precious gift of the Vedic Gods, nor Neidegger's *Sprache* as the "house of being"; *vāc* means mere words or verbal utterances. Language is integrally meshed with the blind drives which turn the wheel of meaningless existence.

Under a few rubrics I would like to suggest how Mādhyamika understands language in its natural setting. There is an initial complication: Mādhyamika uses no one Sanskrit word with a range of meaning comparable to *language*. *Vāc* is used of course, but most often I think in the plural, to refer to verbal utterances. Again the conferring of a name (*abhidhāna*) is set off against what receives the name (*abhidheya*) frequently. The Sanskrit term *prapañca* is perhaps the favourite term but, as I shall suggest, it covers both name and the thing named so it is not a word for language. Another term, *prajñapti* is often used but it betrays rather a Mādhyamika theory of language and is in no sense a general term for language. To speak thematically of language therefore is to import a contemporary concept and problem into Mādhyamika Buddhism -- but I am going to assume that this is legitimate.

The most obvious function of words, the Mādhyamika philosophers think, is to confer names on things. Candrakīrti, in his *Prasannapadā*, draws the boundaries around *duḥkha* (p. 493) or, as he normally calls it, *saṁvṛti*, by saying it is the totality of the transactions of naming and receiving names and of knowing and being known. And he says (p. 364) that only if an object of thought has a specific character can speech (*vācas*) function in relation to it. Naming, however, is not a cool affair of the intellect, a pasting of labels on wine bottles to designate their contents. Far from it. Naming is an integral part of the fear-ridden, kleshic existence in which it appears, serves its purpose and persists. When he is pushed to explain how the notion of self-existence of particular things arises, and after he has shown how untenable the notion is, Candrakīrti explains (p. 264) that it is in order to dispel their apprehension, fears, that men say "things are self-existent" and project the notion of self-existence, so constituting the world of the everyday. Names covering over the abyss of fear, F. Nietzsche would have said. In any case it appears that speaking must serve the purposes of a being caught up in the basic afflictions.

Much becomes clear from the use of the term *prapañca*. It is sometimes taken to mean *language* as it includes name as well as what is named; it is sometimes translated as *phenomena* as it includes the object correlate of a name. Certainly both aspects should be held together and so I translate the term as *named-thing*. As it is most often used as a collective noun like forest or army, I think of it as *the manifold of named-things*: the entire world that can be captured in language and which must be coped with by means of language. Its reference is usually outward; it is the external pole corresponding to the *loka*, the ordinary man;

prapañca is *saṁvṛti* when this is understood as made up of named-things. It is this inseparability of the names of speech and what is named through speech that is characteristic of Mādhyamika. I think we can say that there is no thing without a name: naming and coming into existence within a *loka*, a personal world, are one and the same event with two aspects. Nor can there be names without something named. There are of course empty words like "the horns of a rabbit" but, according to Mādhyamika, no empty names.

At the risk of appearing to retract this very point it must be remembered that no buddhist has ever thought that the things of the everyday -- the commonest recipients of names -- exist *realiter*. They are held to be temporary aggregates of component elements, owing their apparent existence to the ignorance and fears of men. King Milinda's chariot stands as the paradigm of this doctrine. The components of the chariot -- wheels, axles, tongue, etc. -- are held to correspond to their respective names but nothing which can be directly perceived over and above these components corresponds to the word *chariot*. The word *chariot* refers to the assemblage of lesser things -- which would be *parts* if there were anything for them to be parts of. At this level it is clear that the word *chariot* functions differently than the words *wheel*, *axle*, *tongue*, etc. For one thing it *presupposes* them. Only if something is named by such words, can the word *chariot* function, whereas they can function without it. Again, whereas on this level the lesser names function by one-to-one reference, the wheel in question being the sole referent of the name *wheel*, the word *chariot*, having no such referent, functions rather by suggesting, virtually prescribing, certain appropriate ways of dealing with wheels, axles, tongues, etc. When invited to mount into a chariot one does not straddle the tongue nor cling to the wheel. *Chariot* is not a name of something, it is a *prajñapti*, a way of conveying a message.

Now the lesser parts in their turn are obviously as much dependent on their own still lesser parts as the chariot was on them. The buddhist pushes the reduction, as everyone knows, to the level of a small list of irreducible elements, the *dharmas*. These are directly given in either outer or inner perception, mostly the latter, and as they have no parts and so depend on nothing other than themselves, each may properly be named, so most schools supposed, without the use of *prajñapti*. The Mādhyamika refuses to concede this uniqueness, however; in his view *dharmas* too are composite, surreptitiously resting on the notions of a self-existent substance (*svabhāva*) and its attributes. It must follow that *dharmas*, elsewhere ontologically sacrosanct, are as irrevocably *prajñaptis* -- elements of speech -- as are all other putative realities.

The bewildering conclusion is inescapable, though no Mādhyamika, as far as I know, ever formulated it this way, that at no level and at no point does language in fact name anything. It does not *refer*, as we say. Its function is rather to bind together a world which is by nature disjointed and meaningless, and to be the means of moving about with practical effectiveness in it. Language, in short, has no cognitive capacity; its role is instrumental; it suggests what to expect from things and what to do with them: it conducts. Words are guides, they preserve proven ways of coping with things. They are, to risk a neologism, ductal or ducational. A name suggests a way. This is perhaps most strikingly so in the case of the notion of person. Person is a signal instance of *prajñapti*; the names *person,* (*pudgala*) or *I* (*ahaṁkāra*) serve very well to bring order into situations, to arouse expectations, to focus memory, to guide reactions, to lend unity to existence. They are cognitively worthless but this does not hinder their usefulness.

That language in Mādhyamika thought can have no cognitive function becomes even clearer when we consider two further thrusts of Nāgārjuna's analysis: one, that all *dharmas* (putative attributions) are false and two, that the very terms attribute and subject of attribution are unintelligible and hence illusory. Nāgārjuna recalls a statement imputed to Buddha when he formulates (XIII.1), "Whatever is not what it pretends to be is unreal." (*Tan mṛṣā moṣadharma yad*). In this picturesque and, I find, devastating phrase Nāgārjuna thrusts language outside the bounds of truth. Every attribute is by definition purloined, borrowed under false pretense and, as it were, put on display at its false owner's home. Nor is the point merely that attributes are interchanged, mixed up. The falseness lies in anything pretending to own, in full title, attributes which are merely borrowed: pretending to be what it is not. To elude the obvious liar's paradox here Nāgārjuna says the notion of *śūnyatā* must be introduced; but more of that later.

This cardinal point receives a special investigation under the heading "Subject and Attribute" (*lakṣyalakṣaṇam*) (V). Nāgārjuna attempts to convince that both these notions are unintelligible. If you wish to speak of a subject of attribution apart from any attributes you are speaking of nothing; and if the subject is nothing, how can any qualities be attributed to it? End of subject. If you wish to speak of attributes apart from any subject you are attempting to attribute a quality without having anything to attribute it to, to offer a characteristic of what has no character. An attribute must be an attribute *of* or it is not an attribute, whatever else it may be. Now Mādhyamika believes that the cognitive function of language rests on attribution i.e., makes sense only on the model of an epistemic object and what may be predicated of it. It follows that verbal assertions, whatever else they may do for humans, do not serve to know anything in the way in which we ordinarily presume we know something i.e., being able to say what something is.

The final point in the critique (emasculation) of natural language concerns the notion of *is*. The most elementary presumption of an assertive use of language is the notion *is*. If there is no *isness* (*areness*) in things i.e., if things *are* not thus or thus, then assertions about them are adrift in a meaningless ocean of words. Now if there is any one essential view in Mādhyamika it is that the *isness* of things or, lest thing mean only tangible entity the *isness* of any putative ontic existent, including, of course, the phenomena of consciousness, is delusory. Required indeed to constitute an everyday world, an arena for kleshic struggles, *isness* misleads to a delusory sense of the reality of things. Isness, in the form of *svabhāva*, self-existence, makes sense only of the way things truly are (*tattvam*) not of the way they ordinarily are. This thought lies so deep in Mādhyamika thinking that it is the unspoken background to all their arguments. It is explicit in the investigation into self-existence when (XV.6,7) it is said that those who think in terms of *is* and *not is* do not grasp the Buddha's teaching. Buddha is said to be enlightened precisely because he comprehends existence and non-existence in the true way. No doubt is then left that this true way is to avoid using these notions of anything in the everyday world.

THE PROBLEM SKETCHED

Thus the Mādhyamika understanding of ordinary language. Language is born of and serves the timeless need of men to comfort and deceive themselves with a world of pretend reality. It serves an intellectual faculty which is subject to kleshic demands; all reasoning, based on the everyday understanding of language, must fail to be knowledge, must fail to be anything more than sophisticated screams from the seminars and classrooms of *duḥkha*. Śāntideva says quite simply, quite devastatingly, "The intellect and the delusive everyday are one". (*Buddhi: saṁvṛtir ucyate*) (IX.2). Is this the end? If the intellect has condemned itself to be severed from truth is it not trapped in its own flybottle? Are its pronouncements pretending to truth not the babblings of a great infant who draws attention to his wants but is without the faculty to express himself clearly? Is human talk not mere bedlam? And, if it is, should the Mādhyamika, the one who has drawn our attention to this state, not be the first to button up his lips and to withdraw into the horrors of unfulfilled silence?

This places us squarely in front of the central problem of buddhism philosophy, a problem which can be only sketched in its outlines at this time. The buddhist does not restrict himself to a description of kleshic existence (*duḥkha*); his one concern is to put an end to it and so he speaks about the possibility and the nature of a way which would go beyond the natural order; he speaks as if he were already beyond it; yet he does this using natural language. How does he understand his own ability to make language serve the purpose of getting beyond *duḥkha*, to make statements which concern the true way of things? Is he not doomed to absurdity? Must he not demand more of language than his own conception of it will permit? Most especially, how can the Mādhyamika, the severist of sceptics, the buddhist who tells us that verbal utterance is inoperative in ultimate truth (493), extricate himself from his own self-stultifying naturalist views?

One might well, on a first reading of the texts, find an abundance of evidence that Mādhyamika does abandon language to *saṁvṛti* and condemn himself to silence. Candrakīrti refers to the Buddha's night of enlightenment when he uttered not one syllable, being freed from everything with name (539). Nāgārjuna states that the true way of things (*tattvam*) is not expressible through the names for things (*prapancair aprapañcitam*) (XVIII.9); and he argues that it is unintelligible to assign any attribute, drawn from the realm of the *skandhas*, the nameable, to the *tathāgata*, a synonym for the way things are really.

But, by itself, this emphasis would only deepen the absurdity (language drawing a boundary around itself!) and give an unbalanced result. We must, it seems to me, understand Mādhyamika in such a way as to justify its talking about the matters which concern it most. This is, of course, a problem in its own right and demands persistent study of the word and spirit of the texts. At this time I shall merely sketch some of the ways open to us to complete the Mādhyamika philosophy of language, without attempting to be definitive and certainly not exhaustive.

The terms around which a study of this intriguing question must, it seems to me, centre are: 1. *prajñapti* (the non-cognitive nature of words); 2. *śūnyatā* (the absence of being in particulars); 3. *satyadvayam* (the dual context of language); 4. *bodhisattva* (embodied enlightenment).

All names are *prajñaptis*, suggestions of the way thought and behaviour should go; language cannot describe states of affairs yet serves to convey intentions. In a specific Mādhyamika sense, *prajñaptis* are terms which have the power to conduce to entering and proceeding on the buddhist way. Nāgārjuna says this of his own most favoured idea -- *śūnyatā*. "The true way of things we hold to be the devoidness of self-existence in them; this devoidness is a conductal notion (*prajñapti*) presupposing the everyday world; it alone is the middle way." (XXIV.18). When this is placed alongside Candrakīrti's chain of synonyms (p. 264) -- *dharmatā*, *sūnyatā*, *svabhāva*, *tathatā* and *tattvam* -- it seems we may fairly conclude that the entire treasury of preferred buddhist terms, not excluding *buddha* and *nirvāṇa*, are not meant to have cognitive value but function in a conductal way within the buddhist enterprise. Nāgārjuna pronounces, with his usual audacity, "No truth has been taught by a Buddha for anyone, anywhere at any time". Can it be that everyday language, freed from the misconception that it refers to self-existent things, becomes available, in the mouths of the wise, to guide beings in the direction of buddhist freedom?

Śūnyatā, the term which more than any other lures us into the intricacies of Nāgārjuna's thought, is an invitation to proceed through the everyday without treating anything in it as either in being or as illusory. This holds not only for entities but as well for the short list of irreducible reals -- the *dharmas*. *Śūnyatā* has the superficial appearance of nihilism but is intended to open the world to the presence of what is not entity but rather the truth of entities. Words themselves are not real as particulars but are as open to the presence of what is not particular as is any other putative constituent of the everyday world. By nature, then, language is capable of functioning effectively in the dimension of what *transcends* the everyday: because that, whatever it is, has been the true character of both the everyday world and of language from the beginning. It is Nāgārjuna's genius to use the one term *śūnyatā* to evoke the nature of both bondage and freedom, of both the everyday and what resolves it.

We are at this point very close to the notion of the two truths, *satyadvayam*, a notion Mādhyamika makes distinctive use of. The locus classicus is Chapter XXIV of Nāgārjuna's *kārikās*. "The teaching of the Buddhas is wholly based on their being two truths, that of a personal, delusive world and truth in the highest sense." "Those who do not clearly comprehend the due distinction between the two truths cannot clearly know the hidden sense of the Buddha's doctrine." "Except as based on the language of everyday transactions the ultimate truth cannot be pointed out; if the ultimate truth is not grasped, *nirvāṇa* cannot be attained." (XXIV.8.9.10).

The apparent clear cleavage between the two truths might be expected to discourage any attempt to draw on the language of the everyday for purposes of making statements about truth in the highest sense. But the last *kārikā* (XXIV.10) opens another possibility: "except as based on the language of everyday transactions the highest truth cannot be pointed out". It is clear that there is only one language available, that of the everyday, and yet by using it the truth which is beyond the everyday may be pointed out or *taught*. Any word suggesting knowing or description is conspicuously absent from this formulation. Pointing is a behaviour word.

Candrakīrti deals with this problem in a way which contributes something to a discussion of the possibility of metaphysics. Commenting on Nāgārjuna's characterization of the ultimate truth "not dependent on anything other than itself, at peace, not manifested as named-things, beyond thought construction, not of varying form -- this is the true way of things" (XVIII.9), he says, "nonetheless even what lies beyond naming must be characterized drawing on conventional usage by a transfer of terms accepting the conventional assumptions 'this is real', 'this is not real', and so on" (372). This passage, and many others, raises questions of the use of metaphor, analogy, and implicit models at the point where thought struggles to reach into a dimension which appears to be other than the empirical: questions which remain unresolved in spite of millenial concern.

Another Mādhyamika, Āryadeva, earlier than Candrakīrti by three or four hundred years, and immediate successor to Nāgārjuna, has taken up the notion of the two truths in what seems to me to be a more promising way. He says that the two truths are *reciprocally* interdependent as the great and the small (p. 88). Buddha taught the *dharma* basing himself on both the everyday and the superior truth. Both are true and not false if understood in reciprocal dependence. Buddha can say to Ānanda, "go to the town of Śrāvastī and beg your food", without speaking falsely because: 1. his words accord with everyday usage; 2. he knew there was in truth no town, no food, no Ānanda; 3. he used the everyday concepts and words in the interests of Ānanda's enlightenment.

It is false, Āryadeva says, to state that a date fruit is small or that a cucumber is large. But it is not false to claim that a date is smaller than a cucumber nor that this is larger than a date. If this notion is applied to the two truths we may reach some interesting interpretations. Truth in the highest sense, if affirmed in its own terms and without reference to the everyday, is no more true than is everyday truth apart from the clarifying light of the higher. A metaphysics of *śūnyatā* (the higher truth) held to be abstractly *true*, is the purest *saṁvṛti*; it is, by definition, false. All theories are samvritic; there is no second, privileged realm to which philosophical theories refer. Either of the two *truths* taken apart from the other, is false. Only when the lower truth is spoken in the understanding of *śūnyatā* (the higher truth) or when the *śūnyatā* understanding is turned onto the everyday, is what is said *not* false.

Even at this point the puzzle remains: outside of a cognitive context what can it mean to speak of truth and falsehood? The most difficult problems of Mādhyamika thought become discernible here and demand separate and extensive study. My own attempt at penetration would take up the notion of the middle way as a possibility of satisfying the demands of ontology and epistemology, or, as a possibility of carrying on after both ontology and epistemology have been left behind. Nāgārjuna does say that *śūnyatā* is itself the middle way. (XXIV.18). This allows us to think that the middle way is not a path that leads to some goal outside itself, but is itself the goal, integrating and transmuting, somehow, the theoretical and practical into what is both and yet neither. The middle way seems to join the two truths and provide the depths of understanding out of which it is possible to *speak truly, that is, to use words which conduce to enlightenment*.

The *bodhisattva* stands as evidence of the buddhist faith that this is possible. He embodies *śūnyatā;* he does not need the distinction of the two truths; his way is the middle way. Language, which ran headon into the *aporia* of the natural predicament, may recover its evocative power in the mouth of one who has discovered that, despite all the evidence to the contrary, man carries his potence to freedom in himself as a natural being and was never, in truth, caught in a natural predicament.

BIBLIOGRAPHY

1 *Mūlamadhyamikakārikās* de Nāgārjuna avec La Prasannapadā Commentaire de Candrakīrti. Publié par Louis de la Vallée Poussin, St. Petersbourg 1913. Nāgārjuna's Kārikās are indicated by Chapter and number. Thus, (I.1.) indicates Chapter I, Kārikā 1.

2 *Prasannapadā*. Candrakīrti's commentary to Nāgārjuna's Kārikās. All references connected with Candrakīrti are to the text published by de la Vallée Poussin. Thus (1) indicates page 1 of the Prasannapadā.

3 *Bodhicaryāvatāra* of Śāntideva, with the commentary Pañjikā of Prajñākaramati ed. by P.L. Vaidya. Mithila Institute, Darbhanga, 1960.

4 *Śataśāstra* by Āryadeva. *Pre-Dignāga Texts in Buddhist Logic.* G. Tucci.

THE INEFFABLE

By BIMAL KRISHMA MATILAL

"Not a word was uttered by you, O Master,
and (yet) all the disciples were refreshed
by the Dharma-Shower."

(Ascribed to Nāgārjuna, G. Tucci)

"How strange! Under the banyan tree are old men.
Their teacher is only a boy. His explanation
consists in silence. Yet the disciples have been
made free from doubts (through correct understanding)."

(Dakṣiṇamurtistotra, Masson and Patwardhan)

The two verses quoted above are from two different streams of Indian tradition. The first is taken from the tradition of Mahāyāna Buddhism, while the second is from Advaita Vedānta of Samkara. Taken together they present us with the classic, and in every sense, poetic formulation of what I shall call here the *Ineffability* doctrine. Simply stated, the *Ineffability* doctrine means that (a) the Ultimate Reality is ineffable, and (b) the mystical experience in which the Ultimate Reality is supposed to be revealed is also beyond words. The Upanishadic mysticism of ancient India was eloquent about the ineffability of the bliss of Brahman. Thus the Taittinīya says,[1]

Wherefrom words turn back
Along with the mind, without reaching
The bliss of Brahman.

And the Kaṭha notes: [2]

'This is it' - thus they recognize
The highest happiness that is ineffable.

In both these passages, the authors insist that the peak experience in Brahman realization is something that cannot be put into words. It is *too deep* for words.

It seems to be a matter of curious coincidence that the ancient philosophers of religion and the mystics are apparently in agreement with some modern philosophers of language who, under the influence of Lüdwig Wittgenstein, hold to the doctrine of Ineffability in some form or other. It is, however, true that the Western mystics and theologians in the Judeo-Christian tradition propound the *Ineffability* doctrine in the sense that there is something called God or the divine but nothing in principle can be said about its nature. And this is not exactly the same as the position of Wittgenstein in *Tractatus*, according to which, philosophical sentences do not say anything but only "signify what cannot be said, by presenting clearly what can be said".[3] But when we think of the *Ineffability* thesis which has been apparently supported by Nāgārjuna and his followers, it does not seem to be very remote from the contention of Wittgenstein. Āryadeva, disciple of Nāgārjuna, thus contends that although silence (*āryatuṣṇīmbhāva*) is the best method to instruct the Ultimate Reality, philosophic discourses are not entirely useless:[4]

> Just as a *mleccha* (one speaking a foreign tongue) cannot be made to understand by any other language but his own, so also (ordinary) people cannot be made to understand by anything except the conventional language.

In the *Laṅkāvatāra-sūtra*, the Tathāgata says this with the help of a simile:[5]

> Just as a king or merchant (at first) attracts his children with the help of beautiful clay animals for play, and then (at the right time) presents them with real animals, I attract similarly my disciples with various shadow characteristics of the dharmas and then instruct them (when the right time comes) the *Bhūtakoṭi* which is to be experienced by each of them personally.

One is obviously reminded here of the "ladder" analogy of Wittgenstein:[6]

> My propositions serve as elucidations in the following way: anyone who understands me eventually recognizes them as nonsensical, when he has used them - as steps - to climb up beyond. (He must, so to speak, throw away the latter after he has climbed up it.)

Even Diṅnāga, who rejected Nāgārjuna's critique of the *pramāṇa* theory, believed the *svalakṣaṇas* to be ultimately beyond words. This is, at least, how Diṅnāga was interpreted by his later interpretor, Dharmakīrti. To use Diṅnāga's own words, the *svalakṣaṇas* (the ultimate particulars) are self-manifesting *(sva-saṃvedya)*, inexpressible in words *(anirdeśya)* and visible to the respective sense-organs (*indriya-gocaraḥ*).[7] While I concede that Diṅnāga's line admits of alternative interpretations, I wish to point out that at least one of the traditional interpretations believes that for Diṅnāga the *svalakṣaṇas*, which are ultimately real and are revealed in perceptual consciousness, are ineffable. What *can* be seen, *cannot* be said.

Indian philosophers, who hold to the doctrine of Ineffability in some form or other, agree that all philosophic discourses about the Ultimate Reality are provisional, but not useless.

A religious or philosophic discourse, that is based upon a belief on the *Ineffability* thesis is considered by Indian philosophers to be a game or play leading to a goal, but it is to be sure a worthwhile game. There are various means by which this game can be played. Broadly speaking, Indian philosophers resort to three different methods by which they think the notion of the Ineffable ultimate reality may be effectively conveyed. I shall discuss them accordingly.

First, there is the method *via negativa*. This method is familiar to the Western theologians as the negative theology, according to which it is believed that although there is God nothing *affirmative* can be said about its nature. In the Indian tradition, this method is as old as Yājñavalkya of the *Bṛhadāraṇyaka* Upanisad. Yājñavalkya's much-acclaimed method is nick-named *neti neti:* [8]

"This Self is (simply described as) *not, not.*"

Even Nāgārjuna defines *tattva - that-ness* (reality) with the help of this method: [9]

> The characteristic of *tattva - that-ness* is such that it is independent of being instructed by others, not diversified by diversifying speech, devoid of thought-construction, and non-dual (unambiguous) in meaning.

The method, in fact, consists in saying that although no positive characterization of the ultimate reality is possible, a negative characterization may be in order.

An objection to this method will take us deeper into the logical (philosophical) problem of negation. Negation is usually understood as the opposite of affirmation. It is generally presumed that there cannot be any bare negation. Whenever anything is denied, some positive ground of denial is assumed. From this rather trivially true premise, it is sometimes argued that each denial involves us into some form of commitment, some form of positive presupposition. The presupposition may be in the form of assuring the existence of a subject of the denial (as the existence of the subject in the denial, *this is not a pot*). Or it may be in the form of our implicitly assuming some other predicate to be true of the subject (as *red* or *green* in the denial, *the pot is not blue)*.

Indian logicians from very ancient times used to make a distinction between the two types of negation: *paryudāsa - privation of terms* and *prasajya-pratiṣedha - denial of what could have been,* roughly corresponding to the term-negation and propositional negation or denial of a predication. [10] The Sanskrit grammarians rightly noted that formation of Sanskrit compound is allowed generally in the first case, but not in the second. It is also pointed out that positive presupposition is very prominent in the first case, but not so in the second. Bhāvaviveka, a follower of Nāgārjuna, argued that in presenting the Ineffable through *via negative* method the second type of negation was involved. In fact, it would be an extreme form of the second type of negation - a negation where the positive presupposition is practically avoided.[11] The second type of negation, as it was understood by Bhāvaviveka, always played an important role in Buddhist philosophy. Thus, even a follower of Diṅnāga would interpret his *apoha* doctrine as involving negation where the presuppositional ground is suspended.[12] One may further argue that if, in Diṅnāga's system, *svalakṣanas* are ineffable, then it is only natural that a Dinnagian would say that the ineffable *svalakṣaṇas* are presented through this type of *apoha* or double negation. For this will simply be a more sophisticated use of the *via negation* method.

The second method consists in assigning contradictory attributes or predicates to the Ultimate Reality. Mystics of all ages and of all countries are very fond of this method. To quote from ancient Indian sources:

"It is not coarse, not fine, not short, not long."
(Bṛhadāraṇyaka III.8)

"It moves, it moves not, it is far, and it is near"
(Iśa)

The Mādhyamikas, in fact, combine the first, and the second method and expound their doctrine of Emptiness as the *denial* of the fourfold or twofold alternatives. Instead of asserting that the Ultimate Reality is both *A* and not *A*, it is said that it is neither.

The usual objection to this method is that it defies the laws of ordinary logic. This feeling is generally reflected in the slogan: *mysticism defies rationality*. Many things can be said in favour as well as against this contention, but we will not go into them here.[13] Briefly, it may be stated that it is futile to construct a *super logic* in order to justify mysticism. Rather, it may be a reasonable move if we concede that mysticism is concerned with the non-rational, emotive or affective components of the human mind.

The third method consists in the use of metaphor and rhetoric to convey the notion of ineffability. This is not to be confused with the *Ineffability* thesis in Aesthetics, according to which, a work of art succeeds in expressing something (an emotion or feeling) which ordinary language fails to do.[14] Some Indian philosophers of language argue that although the Ultimate Reality is, in principle, ineffable, it can be conveyed through what they call the operation of *lakṣaṇā* - *indicative function of a word*. Indian semantic theory states that a word occurring in a sentence contributes to the sentence-meaning in either of the two ways: if may *express* a meaning (which would be its primary meaning, generally the lexical meaning) or it may *indicate* a meaning (directly or indirectly connected with the lexical meaning). Thus Madhusūdana Sarasvatī argues that words like *Brahman, God,* or *The Ultimate Reality* are not entirely meaningless, for although they cannot, in principle, *express* the ineffable, they can very well *indicate* it through the indicative function of a word.

Critics of this method, however, points out that it is rather odd that a word that lacks any *express* meaning or lexical meaning, in principle, will be able to have an *indicated* meaning. Generally the rule is: when the lexical meaning of a word is incompatible with the intended meaning of the sentence in which it occurs, we resort to its *indicated* or metaphorical meaning (e.g., *the village is on the river)*. Now, if words like *Brahman* mean thorough *indication* the Ineffable, what do they mean directly? Further, what is the relation between this indicated meaning of the word *Brahman* with its direct lexical meaning?

These objections, however, can be answered with some stipulations, but I will not go into them here. The important thing to remember is that the acceptance of the indicative function of a word is not to be treated as a license which will allow us to derive any meaning from the word according to our whims. It is only a device to account for the already understood sentence-meaning, to explain why a successful communication has taken place between the speaker and the listener when such a communication has already taken place. Thus, it is not like the license of Lewis Carroll's Humpty Dumpty in *Alice's Adventures Through the Looking Glass:*

> "When *I* use a word" Humpty Dumpty said in rather a scornful tone, "it means just what I choose it to mean - neither more nor less". "The question is," said Alice, "whether you *can* make words mean different things." "The question is", said Humpty Dumpty, "Which is to be master - that is all."

The question is: whether we can call something Brahman and again claim it to be ineffable.

Let me conclude by showing that the above is not really a logical paradox. In other words, there is a perfectly good interpretation of the Ineffability thesis which is logically unproblematic. One may say, "There is something x or some fact which cannot be put into words," for to say this is not to put x into words. And this statement is not the same as saying "there is some x about which nothing can *literally* be said."

Again, the second statement appears paradoxical only on the surface. If we allow the distinction between the object language and metalanguage then, perhaps, the second version may also be interpreted non-paradoxically.

FOOTNOTES

1. *Taittirīya* 2.4 (Translation E.H. Hume)

2. *Kaṭha* 5.14

3. Wittgenstein, 4.115

4. Quoted by Candrakīrtī, p. 157

5. *Laṅkavatāra-sūtra,* p. 37

6. Wittgenstein, 6-54

7. See Hattori, p. 27

8. *Bṛhadāraṇyaka IV* 4

9. *Madhyamaka-śāstra,* 18.9

10. See Matilal (1968) p. 156-7 I have called the first *nominally bound negative,* and the second *verbally bound negative.*

11. See Matilal (1971) p. 162-5

12. See Herzberger, p. 11-14

13. See Matilal (1975)

14. Ānandavardhana, in the Indian tradition of literary criticism, criticized and rejected the thesis that *Rasa* (aesthetic) experience is ineffable. See Matilal (1975).

BIBLIOGRAPHY

Hattori, M. *Dignāga, On Perception* Cambridge (Mass): Harvard University Press, 1968

Herzberger, H. "Double Negation in Buddhist Logic", *Journal of Indian Philosophy* 3(1975) pp 1-16

Laṅkāvatārā-sūtra Ed. P.L. Vaidya, Darbhanga: Mithila Institute, 1963

Masson, J.L. & Patwardham, M.V. *Aesthetic Rapture* (2 Vols.), Poona: Deccan College, 1970

Matilal, B.K.(1968) *The Navya-nyāya Doctrine of Negation* Cambridge (Mass) Harvard University Press 1968

Matilal, B.K.(1971) *Epistomology, Logic and Grammar in Indian Philosophical Analysis* The Hague: Monton, 1971

Matilal, B.K.(1975) "Mysticism and Reality: Ineffability" *Journal of Indian Philosophy* 3 (1975), Nos. 3 & 4

Nāgārjuna *Madhyamaka-śāstra* with Candrakīrti's Comm. Ed. P.L. Vaidya, Darbhanga: Mithila Institute, 1960

Wittgenstein, L. *Tractatus Logic-Philosophicus* Tr. Pears & McGuinness, London Kegan Paul, 1922

Upanisads: *Eighteen Principal Upanisads* Ed. Limaye & Vadekar Poona: Vaidika Samsodhana Mandala, 1968

INEFFABILITY RECONSIDERED

By Prof. Mahesh Mehta

Ineffability or inexpressibility is generally considered to be a distinctive mark of an intense inward experience called mystical experience of a suprasensuous reality which is also uncharacterizable. Dr. Matilal has ably controverted the dual notion of ineffability with clearness and precision, and has apparently drawn some *fundamental* conclusions therefrom, regarding the mystical experience, as well as its content - the mystical reality itself, and the status of our world in relation to this reality.[1] The issue of ineffability thus covers in his treatment a vast field of inquiry into the mystical experience and the reality of what is mystically experienced. This constitutes the age-old problem of both mysticism and metaphysics. The title of the paper is somewhat neutral, because the point in question is not only the *ineffability* of mystical experience recognized as a direct and immediate and rapturous approach to the inner reality conceived as spiritual, divine or unconditioned, but the validity and value of mysticism as such. Therefore, before the discussion is focussed on ineffability itself, certain observations will be in order in regard to the three crucial questions mentioned above.

1. The argument against the validity of mystical experience has substantially remained the same. It is based on the fact that the mystical experience is a purely subjective mental condition, and therefore cannot claim authenticity for other's acceptance. The experience in question is not a cognitive one or one that involves an epistemic knowledge of the external world, which is verifiable. ". . . No Means of knowledge, except the mystical experience itself (whose validity is under consideration), can establish its existence". A mystic cannot formulate an empirical criterion to validate his personal experience.

The mystical experience by definition is a state of introvertive consciousness. In this respect it bears the closest analogy to an emotional or an aesthetic feeling. ". . . There are, of course, other non-rational, emotive or affective or non-cognitive components of the human mind." The difference between the aesthetic joy and the mystic joy, despite their similarity (as brought out by Viśvanātha in his well-known statement, *brahmāsvāda-sahodaraḥ kāvyānandaḥ*) naturally corresponds to their different objectives bases or sources of inspiration, sensible and non-sensible, which is precisely what makes them easily accessible-acceptable and not-too-easily-accessible-acceptable forms of experience. Aesthetic experience is not a universal phenomenon. Yet we grant it because it is more wide-spread than the mystical experience, and can be repeated or reproduced. The difference in generality and frequency between the aesthetic and the mystic feelings is occasioned by the proximate and remote nature of their artistic and divine stimulants.[2]

The argument against the independent corroboration of the world's respectable mystics deserves consideration. The example of the supernatural creatures to counteract the point of the agreement of the statements of the mystics all over is chosen in order to suit the original contention that the mystical experiences are of the nature of hallucinations or *illusions (!)*, without any reference to their content-correlate, or lacking in objectivity. But let us suppose that we hear reports about some incredible, fantastic feats performed by men at different places, or reports about similar psychic acts evinced by different persons. In both cases, accumulation of occurrences is of value in that it suggests the validity of the acts and their performers. In other words, it becomes a vindication of the possibility and existence of those phenomena, howsoever improbable they might appear to be. Moreover, in case of the other example one can say that in many instances the authors of the myths do not claim an objective reality for their own mythical conceptions and descriptions, as do the mystics. There is no question of any actual observation or experience of such creatures either by the myth-makers or others. (The argument of the parallelism of the poets' expressions can also be met with, but it can be dropped here.) Of course, in the present argument based on the counter-example given, the basic difference between the physical-psychical and the mystical events is at once recognized. The one is palpable, the other is not, as said above. The example does not prove the validity of mystical experience to the same extent that the other example does not disprove the same. The point is that here is a fundamental divergence of views about the mystic phenomena. Therefore, the argument of the convergence of the mystics' testimony does *at least* have a *corroborative* value.

In regard to providing an empirical test to prove the validity of mystical experience, it may be mentioned that Prof. Staal in his recent work, *"Exploring Mysticism - A Methodological Essay"* not only accepts the possibility and authenticity of mystical experiences, but argues that it can be rationally and critically studied. He writes, ". . . This has taken me into mystic domains which are widely regarded as beyond the pale of critical investigation. I argue that they are not, . . ." (p. xv), ". . . a rational, theoretical, as well as experimental, approach to this area is not only possible but necessary if mysticism is ever to become a serious subject of investigation; and that there are, in fact, indications that a theory of mysticism, based in part upon such critical investigation, is promising" (p. 9).[3]

2. The impugning of the phenomenon of mystical experience leads to the fundamental scepticism about the very existence of the ultimate reality. It rests on the assumption that the postulate of such a supramundane reality is accessible only to the mystical experience and is not at all provable on "independent grounds". If the hypothesis of a supersensible reality were to be entirely and exclusively a matter of mystical experience, one would dismiss it or disregard it without much hesitation. It is hardly fair to say that the doctrine of higher reality of the world is not demonstrable or discernible independently and is impervious to reason. The massive and robust history of metaphysical reasoning is an evidence to the contrary. That one may or may not subscribe to those arguments, is beside the point. The fact is that there does exist a domain of thought, in which the search for truth is prosecuted along unbiassed rational and philosophical lines, in which one finds a consistent exercise of ratiocination and analysis. An intellectual tradition of such proportions can be summarily brushed aside not without causing detriment to a significant achievement of the human mind.

Buddha understandably did not attempt to prove the existence of the reality of Nirvana, nor did Nagarjuna and the other Mahayana thinkers *necessarily* establish the concept of ultimate reality called by them *tattva, paramārtha* or *tathatā*. Vendānta seeks to posit the ultimate reality of *ātman-brahman* on the basis of its elaborate and many-sided epistemology and ontology, the pivot of which is the analysis of the concept of consciousness or awareness variously called *cit, samvit,* or *jñapti*, conjoined with the notion of being or *sat*.

Be it as it may, the metaphysical idea of the ultimate reality cannot be relegated to an uncritical faith based on an implicit acknowledgement of the veracity of a subjective experience of a so-called mystic or a seer. To say the least, it is a *reasonably* sound proposition to go by. The issue ultimately boils down to the exciting and everlasting controversy between the proponents of logical positivism mainly contemporary and of ancient and modern metaphysics, both Eastern and Western.

It is also true to say that the verdict of mystic experience per se as regards any extraordinary, unperceivable truth is not actually to be taken seriously, unless it is also capable of being verified and understood by reason and the *pramāṇas* of logic. Robinson writes, ". . . The impulse to logic, not felt while the mystic mood is dominant, reasserts itself as the mood fades." This is the domain of *prstha-labdha-jñāna* -

after-obtained knowledge - or *pratyavekṣaṇā-jñāna* (retrospective knowledge).[4] What precedes, spontaneous intuitive experience or cool reason, cannot always be ascertained. Whether it is one or the other or an *alternation* of both, is not of great moment. The rational attitude is to take cognizance of the entire gamut of human experience - be it intellectual, scientific, psychological, emotional, aesthetic, or mystic, and by a judicious incorporation of the various aspects of experience, one must endeavour to formulate a composite and comprehensive picture of reality.

3. Incumbent on the notion of the ultimacy of the metaphysical reality is the idea of the non-finality of the phenomenal world, especially in the Indian philosophical systems. The realm of this reality, which is in some sense spoken of as supraphenomenal, is by the same token viewed as more real, truer and as the *ne plus ultra*, the most covetable end of all the intellectual and religious efforts of man. The soteriological philosophies of India consistently develop a doctrine of two truths (*satyadvaya*), the empirical and the transcendental; and the transcendent truth is *mokṣa* or *nirvāṇa*, symbolizing the unification with the ultimate reality, whatever it be. This being so, Matilal's objection to this reality being regarded as better, more real, more valuable is quite justifiable from the point of view of his anti-idealistic Nyāya view of the reality of the material and the external world regarded as an *antidote* to mysticism which apparently connives at our normal world of sense.

However, it may be pointed out that the Nyāya is also in the ultimate analysis a soteriological system despite its realism and as such conceives of a supreme state of emancipation for the soul, when the so-called reality and materiality of the world is left behind. The *ātma-dravya,* the most important of the substances, and the substrate of the quality of *jñāna,* knowledge (*jñānādhikaraṇam ātmā*) stands *nirguṇa* in its highest and purest condition, devoid of all qualities including consciousness, which makes the knowledge of the external objective world possible. Thus in *mokṣa*, the self is divested of its inherence of intimate association *(samavāya)* with its quality of cognition, of which the world is an object. The world thus becomes less real, less valuable than the higher unconscious state of the eternal freedom of *ātman* in the Nyāya system.

The Nyāya system also recognizes *yogaja pratyakṣa* as a kind of *alaukika,* extra-ordinary perception. So to a *naiyāyika* mystic who has experienced an undifferenced state of no-consciousness or no-mind, the world is not likely to appear exactly the same when he comes out of his yoga.

It is no doubt true that the *classical* absolutist-monist-idealists of India, the Mādhyamikas, the Yogācāras, and the Kevala-Advaitins felt themselves metaphysically committed to belittle the phenomenal world as unreal, illusory or dream-like in their unmitigated non-dualistic zeal, *though it need not be so*. But, the extremists among the absolutist Mādhyamikas and the Advaita Vedāntins, such as Nāgārjuna, Candrakīrti and Gauḍapāda, Śrīharṣa (the latter following the former's foot-steps) go a step further and are anxious to prove by means of their *prasaṅga* dialectic how hollow, illogical, self-contradictory, incomprehensible, the world-order is. There is much force in the criticism of the Mādhyamika dialectical reasoning presented through Udayana's lively and humorous but apposite argument in his *ātmatattvaviveka*. Yet nowhere is the reality of the material world outright; its qualified reality is recognized in all systems including absolutism.

Nevertheless, it need not be maintained that the absolutist perspective reducing the world of phenomena to a māyic appearance is inseparably tied up with mysticism or its doctrine of ineffability. In other words, the mystical attitude toward the world we live in is not to be entirely identified with the absolutism lending itself to a view, which ultimately evaporates the world into a thin mist. Such a perception of the world is only one of the manifestations of a mystic's realization, which in effect only carries forward a foregone philosophical conception of the mystic concerned. Therefore it is not to be regarded as inevitably germane to mysticism as such.

Evidently, a mystical experience is considered to be a catalyst, since it affords a penetrating insight into the inner reality of one's self. It is essentially a seeing within of the synthetic unity, the true nature of all things. It is said to melt away our habitual adherence to the plurality and polarity of the objective and conceptual prejudices. In the subsequent moment of a mystic's awakening, by virtue of his erstwhile contact with the underlying reality the world presumably stands transformed in his perception. He reviews and regards the same objective reality with a different attitude and value; he is no longer affected by the surface forms of things. Whether the world now appears like a phantasmagoria or like a *thème avec variations*, an illusion (*māyā*) or a play (*līlā*) depends on whether the person's intellectual background is imprinted with the conception of the Absolute or the Divine. It is the transformation or re-visioning that is the hallmark of mystical experience, not necessarily the aspect of illusoriness or unreality of the world.

In the foregoing discussion, the three fundamental questions pertaining to mysticism in general were considered. I will now specifically deal with the notion of ineffability in mysticism. First the ineffability as applied to the mystic feeling and then to the felt reality.

(1) When ineffability is said to be the common denominator of mystical experiences, it is only a metaphorical way of conveying the want of a fully satisfactory description of the intensity and poignancy of the mystic ecstasy. Apart from the fact that inexpressibility is also an expression, it may be pointed out that the mystics were not only not inarticulate or nebulous, but when we take into account their copious utterances abounding in vivid descriptions dressed in noble and beautiful poetic images evoked in tranquil moments following their own experience of deepened or elevated consciousness, one begins to wonder how mystical experience can be regarded as completely ineffable. However, Matilal writes, ". . . if a mystic claims that his mystical experience is certainly valuable but it is ineffable, his position is like that of the jeweller who says that he can set a value on a particular jewel but cannot tell why he sets that particular value on that particular jewel. Or, we can say that the mystic is like a poet who has not uttered a word but claims to have written a very beautiful poem."

There can be no hesitation in concurring with Ānandavardhana when he demonstrates that the *rasa*-experience of an aesthete cannot be said to be ineffable, "since ineffability in the sense that something is beyond the reach of all words, is impossible." The disagreement arises, when a distinction is drawn between the emotional experience and the mystical experience, and the latter regarded to be utterly mute. What is meant to be emphasized here is that what applies to the aesthetic experience holds good for the mystical experience as well; both are fervent inner feelings. (Their objective difference shown above is not significant here.) Therefore, it is not right to say that the aesthetic experience is not absolutely ineffable and the mystical experience is absolutely ineffable, and further because the mystics are not incapable of expressing their experiences as the records of their words amply prove. Moreover, there is a minor discrepancy involved in putting an aesthete's and a mystic's experiences together. The proper juxtaposition would be that of a poet (and not an aesthete) and a mystic. A poet's aesthetic experience is original and creative as distinguished from an aesthete (*rasika sahṛdaya*)'s appreciative(and perhaps recreative) experience. Likewise, a mystic's spiritual experience is original and also creative. A poet and a mystic, although different, are sometimes hardly distinguishable; there can be a mystical poet and a poetic mystic. The upshot of the discussion is that if a poet's experience is, as we all know, so expressible (or even an aesthete's experience for that matter is not entirely ineffable *a la* Ānandavardhana), there is no reason why a mystic's experience should be described as totally ineffable. If Anandavardhana were asked about the mystic experience, he would in all probability, say, "it is not beyond the reach of *all* words." In short, ineffability is not to be understood literally; it is to be understood in a qualified sense as said in the beginning of this point. Experience, joyful or painful, exceeds expression (*daśāṅgulam atitiṣṭhati*), does not exclude it. Communicability is especially imperfect in the case of moving and powerful experiences impinging on our normal consciousness - be they mystical, artistic, aesthetic, emotional or sensual.

(2) At the outset, it must be said that the above discussed three issues of a fundamental nature appear to have been derived from the discussion of ineffability based on an analysis of the three methods adopted by the absolutist thinkers to communicate their reality, though the connection between the two is not very apparent. The exposition of ineffability doctrine pervades both ontological and epistemological absolutisms, such as those of the older Upaniṣads and Śaṅkara leading to Madhusūdana, and of Nāgārjuna, Vasubandhu, and Dinnāga-Dharmakīrti.

Nevertheless, the contention against the doctrine of ineffability lies implicitly in another direction. Karl Potter coined a term "linguaphobia"[6] to describe the absolutist (linguaphobe)'s concern for the indescribability of his reality, epistemic or ontic, and his aversion to use language which derives from discursive, dichotomous knowledge. Conceptualization (*vikalpa*) and verbalization (*prapañca*) go hand in hand. There is reason to believe that ineffability is equated with linguaphobia by Matilal. It is the Advaita Vedāntic and Mahāyāna Buddhist systems of absolutism that are designated and discussed under the rubric of these terms. Indescribability or indeterminability is the inevitable logical outcome of the conception of the non-dual, transcendental reality in absolutism.

There are two ways in which ineffability can be understood. Firstly, it can be literally understood to mean utter impossibility of any description which is what "linguaphobia" seems to imply. Linguaphobia is not only a stronger term for ineffability, it is somewhat misleading. The absolutist systems do not shun language; they only stress the inadequacy of language to cope with their reality. It does not preclude talking about the transcendent principle, otherwise all philosophical discourse would be non-existent. Hence ineffability may be re-defined to mean an inability to do justice linguistically to the absolute integrity of the reality, which consists in its non-conceptual non-polarity. Thought or language cannot escape polarity. All predication is but a useful, even indispensable, approximation.

All terms, both positive and negative, such as *sat*, *brahman*, *nirguṇa*, *tathatā*, *neti neti*, *śūnyatā*, etc. etc. are accepted as the necessary conceptual instruments for the comprehension of reality. This certainly does not involve any disparagement of language or rational thought.[7] Although in reality, both thought and language are outdistanced (*yato vāco nivartante aprāpya manasā saha)* by the Ultimate, none of them are abandoned altogether at the rational level.

Really speaking, we cannot make too much capital out of inexpressibility; expression is legitimate and permissible in absolutism. However, we have to make allowance for the degree of difference in regard to the use of language in Buddhist absolutism and Vedāntic absolutism. The latter is not opposed to the ascription of affirming characteristics to the absolute reality. The negative mode is apparently more convenient. But, in the final analysis, from the point of view of the reality itself both are left behind, because both are maintained by a dualistic reference. To put it in a slightly different way, Advaita does not reject positive linguistic formulation for the ultimate reality, though it accepts it in a diminishing order. It admits of clearly dualistic descriptions where it joins hands with the personal, theistic (*saguṇa)* traditions. Then comes an abstract representation of pure, unitary attributes, then a negative representation, and then . To illustrate, all-knowingness *(sarvajñatā)* is an epistemic-dualistic quality, knowledge *(jñāna)* is pure, undivided but it is still in relation to its opposite, then beyond knowledge *(nirguṇa, nirvikalpa, neti neti)*, and finally *(peace, śānta)*. When mind is denuded of its congnitions and words are relieved of their antinomies, when all the conceptual and verbal constructs *(vikalpas)* cease,[8] the contemplative absorption into the transcendent *tattva* takes place in the profound silence of the plenitude of one's being. Interestingly enough, in *speaking* of silence we run into a real logical impasse, which we can never get out of.

It cannot be denied that there are occasional references to the complete unnameability and unspeakability of reality[9] in the absolutist systems. This speechlessness is called eloquent silence *(maunam eva vyākhyānam)*, because it exactly characterizes the reality, whose nature is quiescence *(upaśama)* of all that we can conceive of. It is regarded as the most appropriate way to represent the reality,[10] because as soon as a mystic opens his mouth he is caught in the network of constructs. However, he may take recourse to the superimposition of conceptual characteristics on the "wordless" for the purposes of communication *(śruyate deśyate cāpi samāropat anakṣaraḥ)*[11] Śaṅkara describes Lord Dakṣiṇāmūrti as *maunena manda-smita-bhūṣitena maharṣilokasya tamo nudantam* (dispelling the darkness of the great sages by his deep silence tinged with a gentle, beauteous smile). The Divine Teacher is not given to unconcerned, self-absorbed reticence; he reveals a vibrant, communicative calmness rippling with joyful grace. It touches and enlightens those who stand delicately on the verge. The teacher discourses through silence, but the pupil is freed from the doubts *(śiṣyas tu chinna-saṃśayah)*.

This point brings us to the relationship of language and experience, which is the second possible and plausible meaning of ineffability. Its discussion is deferred in order to mention a few points connected with the present issue.

It should be acknowledged, however, that Matilal does not incline to an extreme view of ineffability, though he inclines to consider it as an expression of an unenthusiastic attitude towards language on the part of the absolutists. Consequently, the three methods resorted to by them in their statement about the reality envisaged by them, are delineated to show the sparing use of language for their reality. These methods, the negative, the paradoxical and the indicative are not exhaustive, inasmuch as the analogical and the positive methods of description are omitted.

The *via negativa* or the *neti neti* method denies all predications of the reality. Matilal mentions two types of negation, *paryudāsa* or choice negation and *prasajya-pratiṣedha* or exclusion negation. The latter is relevant here. In the Mādhyamika system, it *primarily* plays its role by annulling all the possible logical alternatives including the mutually contradictory ones in regard to any particular view about the empirical world. On the other hand, speaking in terms of Bhāvaviveka's view mentioned by Matilal it implies no positive epithets, when applied to the ultimate reality. Thus, *prasajya-pratiṣedha* is intended to perform important philosophical functions in the two domains of truth (*saṃvṛti-satya* and *paramārtha-satya*) in the Mādhyamika *absolutism*, in which there can obviously be no question of bare negation. In the empirical sphere, it is not to be viewed as a blank denial of everything whatsoever. When both the logical opposites are *dialectically cancelled*, it breaks the ground for the emergence of the absolute reality. "The Absolute or Nirvāṇa may actually be said to embody the negation of all predicates (or characteristics), in this extreme sense of negation. When alternatives are denied, *emptiness* prevails." [12] In the realm of the ultimate truth, it presents the absolute reality in its suchness *(tathatā)* the dual contradistinctions of thought being *conceptually transcended*. An explanation along the same lines holds good for the role of *apoha* or the method of exclusion in relation to the reality called *svalakṣana* or unique particular in Dinnāga's system.

The paradoxical method needs to be qualified. "The usual objection to this method is that it defies the laws of ordinary logic. This feeling is generally reflected in the slogan: *mysticism defies rationality*" ("The Ineffable"). The law defied is the law of noncontradiction. However, the method does not consist in "bestowing contradictory attributes or predicates", if the phrase means a violation of the logical principle of noncontradiction. The contradictions seen in the Upaniṣadic passages are all explainable in different contexts; they are only apparent contradictions *(virodha-ābhāsa)*, no real *coincidentia oppositorum*.[13] Stace's point of "essential paradoxicality" or irrationality of mystical consciousness is misconceived. Matilal rebuts it. Expressions such as superlogic or nonlogic used to characterize the uniqueness of mystical experience hardly do justice to it. Matilal rightly says, "There is no superlogic. There is only one kind of logic, namely the logic described by the logicians." ". . . it is futile to construct a superlogic in order to justify mysticism" ("The Ineffable"). Even granting for argument's sake that the mystics rationalize their *prior* experience, their talk has to conform with logic, otherwise it cannot hope to receive the kind of serious investigation it does from us. The paradoxical expression adopted by the seers is only a picturesque device to produce a sense of puzzlement, to tease or to jolt one out of one's logical rigidity. Thus, ultimately the paradoxical descriptions become positive, when understood from the different points of view. (*Vide* Śaṅkara's commentary on Īśa Upaniṣad, 5.) It may also be mentioned that even the negative dialectic of the Mādhyamika does not oppose the law of noncontradiction, because there is no co-existence of contradictory propositions involved therein.

In any case, it is the absolutist type of mysticism that follows the *via negativa* to bring out the unutterability of its ultimate reality, Brahman or Śūnyatā (Emptiness, Void). The nonabsolutist, theistic systems simply make short of ineffability; they actually rejoice in showering epithets after epithets on their divine being. Ineffability cannot be called the characteristic of the reality of mystical experience as a whole. Moreover, one fails to see how absolutists can also be accused of avoiding language and expression, when the three methods are accepted by them, not to mention the other two (indicated above) in their talk about the absolute.

It is actually the third method that a special attention

should be devoted to. The real and specific target of criticism is the method of indication used by Madhusūdana,[14] who touches off a delightfully subtle point of reasoning.

The basis of the argument, succinctly stated, is the distinction made in Sanskrit aesthetics between the two powers of a word, the primary or expressive power (*abhidhā-śakti*) and the secondary or indicative power (*lakṣaṇā-śakti)*. A word invariably denotes primarily a particular meaning. Only when this denoted meaning (*vācyārtha, mukhyārtha*) is not feasible, it is to be abandoned and replaced by the indicated meaning (*lakṣyārtha*) connected with the original meaning.

According to Madhusūdana, Brahman, being without any characteristics *(dharmas)* and unknowable (by ordinary means) is not *directly denoted* by such terms as "Truth, Being, Knowledge, Bliss, Infinity", usually applied to Brahman, but only *indirectly indicated*. This is so, because in this case the ground for the application of the denotative function (*pravṛtti*) of these words does not obtain. The idea is: a word, ordinarily, has a cognitive function. Verbal cognition (*śābda-bodha*) takes place, when an uttered word refers to or denotes an objective entity having qualities. But the above words do not express Brahman the way other terms do, because Brahman is not an empirically, cognitively apprehended object; it is qualityless *(nirdharmaka)*. Therefore, these words mean Brahman through indication or indirection (*lakṣaṇā*)

Details of Matilal's clear exposition of his criticism of Madhusūdana's argument (which, in fact, constitutes the latter's *pūrvapakṣa)* need not be repeated. The gist of the counter-argument is: If the terms, *sat, cit, ānanda* indicate Brahman, how do you account for the lack of direct denotation of these terms? Without the prior exercise of the denotative power of a word the indicative power cannot be evoked. Thus, Madhusūdana violates the principle of *lakṣaṇā*. He skips *abhidhā,* the primary, expressive level and reduces the role of such terms to mere *indirect pointing* rather than direct conveying (cf. arundhatī-darśana-nyāya). This is tantamount to robbing language of its cognitive function.

The criticism overlooks the fact that, 1) in general, Madhusudana is not *at all* likely to overlook the patent rule of the operation and order of *lakṣaṇā* in relation to *abhidhā,* 2) he states explicitly, ". . . because of the function of the indicated meaning being dependent on the absence of the expressed meaning", [15] and 3) he does *not* really incur the fault imputed to him, because he repeatedly says to the effect that the expressed sense is set aside as incompatible because Brahman is without attributes. (Actually, this reason is also to be found in Matilal's citation of Madhusūdana.) To explain: It is not that the *mukhyārtha* is not at all generated and *lakṣyārtha* directly comes into action. Those terms signifying attributes denote Brahman all right. But, if this denoted meaning were to coincide with the nature of reality, the signification of the terms would stop there and Brahman would be imagined as a reality susceptible to attributes and predications, whereas Brahman is *nirdharmaka*, attributeless. These *dharmas* are relative to and contingent on their logical-conceptual counterparts, and Brahman is relationless, absolute in Advaita (*nirupādhika, nirviśeṣa, nirvikalpaka)*. Under the circumstances then, the primary meaning has to give way *(nirdharmakatayā vācyatvabādhāt)* to the secondary meaning of the non-duality of reality (*brahma-rūpavyaki-lakṣakatayā).*[16] So, here we have a two-level reference. The attributive terms refer to *sadharmaka brahma* by denotation and to *nirdharmaka brahma* by indication. Both the meanings are related by, say, contingence *(sāpekṣatā)*; the relatedness *(saṃbhanda)* of the two *arthas* is an important requisite of *lakṣaṇā*. It may be added that by the same token the *suggestion (dhvani)* is that the negative terms *nirdharmaka* etc. are also in the final analysis to be regarded in the same way being subject to the same reasoning. All terms, positive or negative, (including Brahman or Śūnyatā) are ultimately pointers, symbols of the reality stripped of all thought-constructions.

Madhusudana gives another ground for *lakṣaṇā*. The terms in question cannot stop at discharging their cognitive function also because of Brahman's non-cognizability (*avedyata)* by the ordinary means of knowledge. This *pramāna-avedyatā* points to *pratyātma-vedyatā* (intuitive, experiential knowability). Madhusudana introduces an identical piece of argument about Indication in *Siddhāntabindu,* his commentary on Śaṅkara's *Daśaślikī*.[17] He says in essence, "The undifferenced, non-conceptual, non-cognitive *(nirvikalpaka)* apprehension of the meaning of a sentence (such as, *tat tvam asi*) is Knowledge *(pramā)*. The mere verbal cognition does not bring about fulfilment *(kṛtakṛtyatā)*, "because of the content of knowledge being concealed and dualistic." - This leads us to the forthcoming and final point of this study.

In conclusion, the particular difficulty raised against Madhusūdana's argument of the non-*expressibility* of reality is thus obviated. The flaw of omission (of direct meaning) or the charge of "license" cannot be levelled against his point that the terms have an indirect, indicative purport in the case of the ultimate reality. Matilal's pointing out the relevant passage in the *Advaitasiddhi* for his specific criticism of ineffability based on the method of indication is commendable; the criticism, however, misses the point in Madhusūdana's argument.

The entire discussion centering around the idea of ineffability has resulted in a fundamental difference of perspective. On the one hand, its criticism is widened so as to throw doubt on the validity of mystical experience, the reality of what is experienced, and its value. On the other hand, it is possible to show that ineffability is to be understood with *important qualifications*, and also that it is integrally involved in the *experience* of reality as such, and expecially in the nature of *absolute* reality, and this reality is *ipso facto* the ultimate value. Seen in this light ineffability is not a *dūṣaṇa* (fault), but a *bhūṣaṇa* (merit)!

Finally, the rationale for the absolutist's cautious attitude towards language is this: Our employment of language necessarily falls back on our familiarity with the diversity and duality of mundane experience and mental manipulation. Hence there results a tension between the relative language and the non-dual reality beyond phenomena. Within the framework imposed by the phenomenal order of which concepts and speech are the most significant components, if one plays the intellectual game it can lead to a *progressus ad infinitum*. *Neti neti* is a token of this perpetual affair with conceptual categories and their relations. Reason is antinomian, language is referential. They are not a substitute of the direct experience of any reality, sensible or otherwise. Such a difference is implicit in the very order of things. It does not imply any detraction of reason or language. If the eagle cannot swim in water, it is hardly his limitation. At the same time, it is also understandable that they have to avail of an appropriate apparatus for the realization of the subtle metacosmic reality. In the entire process of grasping the ultimate truth, the instrumentality of rational thought and linguistic expression is invaluable. They act as sure pointers to the truth.[18] Reason accompanied by speech comes like a dawn heralding the advent of the sun and disappears when the sun bursts forth. They are transcended in the immediacy of the identity with the truth arrived at through them. Intimate contact with the inner reality *(aparoksa-anubhūti)* does not negate or run counter to reason, it is a culmination and maturation of reason. Intellect is illuminative, intuition is unitive. For the same reason, insight is not an infantile or an infra-rational consciousness; in fact, rational impulse gains its consolidation and confirmation.[19] The progression is achieved in and through the empirical-rational knowledge and experience. The phenomenality of the world is rationally transcended, not unrealistically ignored. Mystical experience is thus a complement of metaphysics. Reason martyrs itself to return renewed after realization. Mystical consciousness, if anything, effects an expansion, an efflorescence of one's already present noetic consciousness.[20] When *vijñāna* (discriminative analytic reason) becomes free from all ideal constructs, it is *prajñāna* (intensive synthetic knowledge).

The absolutist thinkers, when they tend to go beyond thought and speech after they have had their full play, seek to emphasize the experientiality, the direct cognition of their reality. Positively speaking, ineffability is not an expression of fear or antipathy towards language, but becomes a device to nudge one out of his complacence to remain at the verbal level and to awaken him to an insightful integration with the reality.

N O T E S

*This article is developed originally from what was my response to Professor Matilal's extensive article entitled "Ineffability" distributed to the participants of the seminar, and now published in *Journal of Indian Philosophy* (3 (1975), Nos. 3 & 4) under the caption "Mysticism and Reality: Ineffability". Exact page references to this article had to be avoided for practical reasons. The article included in the present volume, "The Ineffable" which was read at the seminar is complementary to the first named article. Since both the writings jointly become a good specimen of Dr. Matilal's thesis and argument against the doctrine of ineffability in mysticism and also some fundamental aspects of mysticism itself, I have thought it advisable to take both into account in the interest of the issue itself, and to attempt to clarify and defend the notion of ineffability in respect of the quandaries posed by Matilal. *vāde vāde jāyate tattvabodhaḥ* (Every discussion brings us closer to the comprehension of truth.)

FOOTNOTES

1. "Since the validity of the mystical experience is in question here. . . . ";

   "Whether such a separate reality (i.e. ultimate reality that is beyond or behind the ordinary everyday world) exists or not, we cannot tell.";

   ". . . the notion of the Ultimate Reality or a supersensible world as well as - the claim that such a world is more REAL or even more VALUABLE than the ordinary world. . . ."

2. Incidentally it may be mentioned that in medieval Bengāl Kṛṣṇaism of the Caitanya school, there is developed an aesthetics of *bhakti*. In it the divine afflatus is considered to be as concrete as aesthetic delight.

3. ". . . the apparently most irrational, most extraordinary, and least accessible manifestations of the soul, that is, its mystical properties, are amenable to rational analysis . . . ." (p. 19) ". . . the study of mysticism is at least in part the study of certain specific aspects of the mind, mysticism and mystical experience cannot be understood in isolation from the more general problem of the nature of mind. Conversely, no theory of mind which cannot account for mystical experience can be adequate" (p. 198).-F. Staal (California, 1975)

   "Many characteristics of clinically induced altered states of consciousness (by researchers) bear a decided resemblance to the characteristics (or noetic qualities) traditionally predicative of mystic experience." (Dr. Herman F. Šuligoj, "Mysticism: A Psychological Structure, and some Epistemological and Metaphysical Implications", read at the CSSR meeting, University Laval, May 1976.) The likeness of drug-induced state of altered consciousness and mystic consciousness is utilized, only because it provides an opportunity of systematically observing the extra-sensory phenomena and being able to throw some light on the obscurity that surrounds mystical occurrences.

   An interesting argument on equal terms is made against the rationalists by F. Schuon. "In connection with the questions raised . . . by the assurance displayed by the negators of the supernatural - who deny others any right to a similar assurance without having access to their elements of certainty - we would say that the fact that the contemplative may find it impossible to furnish proof of his knowledge in no wise proves the nonexistence of that knowledge, any more that the the spiritual unawareness of the rationalist does away with the falseness of his denials.

. . . the fact that a madman does not know that he is mad is obviously no proof to the contrary, just as, inversely, the fact that a man of sound mind cannot prove to a madman that his mind is sound in no way proves it to be unsound." (*Logic and Transcendence* (New York, 1975), p. 66.)

An additional argument of a non-philosophical nature may also be adduced. It is drawn from the point of *vyutthita avasthā* (awakened condition), when a mystic returns to the world of humanity. The saintly attitude characterized by equanimity and loving kindness is also the visible criterion of a holy man, who is said to have a genuine mystical experience and not a passing fantasy, although his experience is not directly accessible to others. The two states of a yogin, the inward and the outward are not discontinuous or incomparable. They are both processes of an identical consciousness, facets of the same truth-realization. The *ātma-sākṣātkāra* in *samādhi*, absorption into the undivided unity of Self, or *prajñā*, insight into the *śūnyatā* of all phenomena, now becomes evident in the conduct of a *jivanmukta sthitaprajña* or a *bodhisattva*, imbued with all-consuming altuistic compassion and selfless service of his fellowmen (cf. four cardinal virtues, *brahmavihāras* or *bhāvanās, maitrī, karuṇā, muditā, upekṣā*). This argument is based on the solid evidence of the ethical thought of the Hindu, Jaina and Buddhist traditions of what may be called *integral* yoga.

4. *Early Mādhyamika in India and China* (Wisconsin, 1967), p. 13 "Of the reality or unreality of the mystic's world I know nothing. I have no wish to deny it, nor even to declare that the insight which reveals it is not a genuine insight. What I do wish to maintain - and it is here that the scientific attitude becomes imperative - is that insight, untested and unsupported, is an insufficient guarantee of truth, in spite of the fact that much of the most important truth is first suggested by its means. . . . Instinct, intuition, or insight is what first leads to the beliefs which subsequent reason confirms or confutes; ... Reason is a harmonizing, controlling force rather than a creative one. Even in the most purely logical realm, it is insight that first arrives at what is new." (Bertrand Russell, *Mysticism and Logic*, (Pelican, 1953)(pp. 18-19.)

5. *duḥkha-janma-pravṛtti-doṣa-mithyajñān-ānām uttorottarāpāye tadānantarāpāyāt apaγargaḥ, Nyāyas ū tras*, 1. 1. 2. Pain, birth, activity, faults and erroneous knowledge - on the destruction of the subsequent ones leading to the destruction of the antecedent, release results.

6. "Linguaphobic Epistemology in India: An Appraisal", circulated in the conference on Philosophy and Language in India, University of Toronto, Sept. 1974.
7. "Another dominant idea of all mystical philosophers is the idea of the inexpressible. The Ultimate is inexpressible, but can be presumably grasped by direct intuition. . . . if the moral of all this is that our comprehension or thought always outruns our language by which we tend to represent what we comprehend, this has a great educative value in philosophy. This can also be taken to be a good challenge to modify, clarify and reorganize our philosophical theories. But if we interpret this (wrongly, I hold) to mean that we should abandon in despair all attempts at reasoned analysis, then we all find ourselves serving as impoverished mourners at philosophy's funeral." (Matilal, *Epistemology, Logic and Grammer in Indian Philosophical Analysis* (Mouton, 1971), p. 167.) A very reasonable statement indeed! Incidentally, Matilal's present study seems to be a sequel to these concluding remarks.
8. ". . . when the cognitive field of thought is laid to rest, nameables are laid to rest, that is, conceptualization is halted, the mental monologue stops, and one knows without superimposing a verbal commentary." (Robinson, *Chapters in Indian Civilization* (Iowa, 1970), pp. 209-210.)
9. *paramārtho hi āryānām tūsnimbhāvah. Madhyamakaśāstra*, XVIII, 7ab, 9ab, XXV. 24
10. ". . . in music the pauses are as essential as the notes." (K. Klostermaier, "The Creative Function of the Word".)
11. *Madhyamakaśāstra*, ed. P.L. Vaidya (The Mithila Institute), p. 115.
12. Matilal, p. 164; Murti, *The Central Philosophy of Buddhism*, p. 234.
13. Staal, pp. 5, 40.
14. *Advaitasiddhi* (Nirnaya Saraya edition), pp. 784-87.
15. Also, *avācyatve lakṣyatva-anupattih*
16. *Laghucandrikā*, a commentary on Advaitasiddhi, trenchantly remarks, "What is conceived to be the substrate of being-ness (*sattā*) is imagined to be subsisting in Brahman, the Pure, Non-dual Being (*paramārtha-sat*). So the latter also becomes subject to the common designation of being the substrate of *sattā*. But, in reality, it is not so; It is non-temporal, impartite Being itself."
17. Chowkhamba (Kashi Sanskrit Series, No. 65), pp. 49-73.
18. Professor Sprung in "Non-cognitive Language in Mādhyamika Buddhism" says to the effect that language has no cognitive capacity and its role is instrumental. Words are guides

(*prajñaptis*): they are "ductal or ducational", because they conduct. They are not in themselves experiential, apprehensional, or in Sprung's terminology, cognitive; they *lead* to the "existential realization" of things. The point is, whether a word reflects, reveals or mirrors reality, evokes a mental cognition, points to its referent or virtually reconstructs reality, it has a "contingent significance". ". . . truth is not to be attained by manipulating utterances but by going beyond the utterances to the experiences towards which they point. The meaning is not to be found in the utterance, but in its object of reference. *Prajñapti* (designation) means a signal, directions or instructions. It is contingent significance as contrasted with inherent meaning. Since the words do not possess intrinsic meanings, the rationalist project of arriving at metaphysical truth by extracting the true meanings of terms is foredoomed. These statements . . . are not intended as the last stage in a rational apprehension but rather as the point of departure for existential realization, not as the moon but as a finger pointing at the moon." (Robinson, *Chapters*, pp. 205, 204)

19. "Their (of the terms "mystical" and "mysticism") association with the idea of the "irrational" is clearly false; spiritual intuition is not irrational but suprational." (Schuon, p.2)

20. "Mystic consciousness does not change the basically rational operability of the mnemomic continuum of experience, but it does allow it to expand its criteria of truth in epistemology, and its understanding of being . . . ." (Šuligoj)

Is Reconstruction from Tibetan into Sanskrit Possible?

By LESLIE S. KAWAMURA

Alexander Csoma de Körös, the fore-runner of Tibetan studies in the West, once wrote:

> . . . Tibet being considered as the headquarters of Buddhism in the present age, these elementary works [i.e. his dictionary] may serve as keys to unlock the immense volumes, (faithful translations of the Sanskrit text), which are still to be found in that country.[1]

He goes on to say:

> . . . The result of this investigation has been that the literature of Tibet is entirely of Indian origin.[2]

The latter statement may reflect the extent of scholarship achieved in the period in which it was written, but at the present time, it has no validity at all. However, in spite of the fact that Tibetan studies has progressed a long way since Alexander Csoma de Körös' time, it is not uncommon to find many modern Buddhist scholars still adhering to the naive belief held by him.

In the light of many indigenous Tibetan texts made available to us, we are now in a more favorable position to accept the fact that the "literature of Tibet" *is not entirely* of Indian origin. Although it may be argued that the availability of Tibetan texts was not as abundant in those days, still a belief such as the one held by Csoma de Körös was quite erroneous in that, such Buddhist schools as, for example, the rNying-ma-pa and the Sa-skya-pa, which have no counterpart in India, were actively flourishing in Tibet in his days. It may have been the case that his contacts were mainly with the dGe-lugs-pa.

Now, the belief that a body of texts written in the Tibetan language is in its entirety of Indian origin and consists, therefore, of faithful translations of the Sanskrit texts has given the Sanskrit language a special status among scholars of Buddhism. This belief has been adhered to even up to the present and one can conclude that it is a common belief among Buddhist scholars that literary Tibetan was invented to accommodate the work of translating Sanskrit texts into Tibetan. Although this conclusion is not altogether wrong, it has been the source for misunderstanding the importance of the Tibetan language as representing an indigenous Tibetan culture of its own. Therefore, scholars have been of the opinion that materials written in the Tibetan language reflected merely the Indian philosophical and psychological systems. Nothing could be farther away from the truth. Were we to accept such an opinion, we not only could not accept a Buddhism in Tibet which has characteristics different from those of India, but also, we could not account for differences, both in theory and in practice, which resulted as a matter of course during the development of Buddhism in Tibet. In other words, we could not account for a Buddhism unique to Tibet.

Much of the misunderstanding stems from three basic sources:

I. The manner in which the literary Tibetan language came about,

II. A certain consistency in the translation of major technical terms, and

III. A belief that anything connected with Tibetan Buddhism has its origin in India.

I. *The Manner in which the Literary Tibetan Language Came About.*

Everyone present here today is aware of the manner in which literary Tibetan language came about. However, just to refresh your memory, I shall quote from S.C. Das' book, *Contribution on the Religion and History of Tibet,* in which he states:

> . . . Srong-tsan gam-po [born 600-617 A.D.] . . . clearly saw that a written language was most essential to the establishment of religion, and more particularly to the institution of laws for the good of the people, and that as long as this all important want remained unsupplied, no success in either could be insured. He, therefore, sent Sambhoṭa, son of Anu, with sixteen companions, to study carefully the Sanskrit language and thereby obtain access to the sacred literature of the Indian Buddhists. He also instructed them to devise means for the invention of a written language for Tibet by adapting the Sanskrit alphabet to the phonetic pecularities of the Tibetan dialect. . . . After returning to Tibet, they . . . framed the system of Tibetan characters, *viz.,* the U-chan or "letters provided with heads" adapted from the Devanāgarī, and U-med, or "headless" from the Wartu, and thus introduced a copious system of written language into Tibet.[3]

This event which took place during the seventh century has led scholars to believe that Tibet was a country which did not have an intellectual tradition prior to the introduction of Buddhism into Tibet. However, there existed at that time, a highly developed spoken language which included sophisticated concepts of indigenous or non-Indian origin. An investigation into the early period of Tibetan history suggests that the Tibetans were not as primitive as some historians will have us believe.[4] In fact, just as Confucian and Taoistic influences help mold Buddhism on Chinese soil, we can safely assume that Buddhism in Tibet was not totally free of Bon influences.[5]

However, getting back to the main stream of thought, because the literary Tibetan language had borrowed to a great extent from the Indian languages, scholars have assumed that Tibetan texts were merely a reflection of the Sanskrit. The revisors and editors to Sarat Chandra Das' *Tibetan English Dictionary* however, were aware that the Tibetans had an indigenous literature of their own. In their *Preface* to Das' dictionary, Graham Sandberg and William Heyde wrote:

> . . . hereto European scholars seem to have thought of the literature of Tibet as one consisting wholly of Sanskritic translations and as limited to the contents of the *Kahgyur* and *Tangyur*. The author and the Revisors have endeavored . . . to show how extensive a field is covered by medieval and modern Tibetan writers. Geography, history, biography, political government, accounts, astrology, are all represented.[6]

Further, W.Y. Evans-Wentz had noticed that, although the Tibetans depended upon the Sanskrit language for their literary language, they were not translating Sanskrit terms lexically, but were making interpretations of the terms in view of setting up a systematic religious system. Evans-Wentz wrote:

> . . . the sanskrit word *Nirvāṇa* literally means *going out* or *blowing out* like the going out of a fire, or like the blowing out of the flame of a candle. It also means *cooling*, or *becoming cool*, with respect to sensuous existence. And Occidentals who have comprehended no more than the exoteric aspects of its meaning have been responsible for the erroneous opinion, now so widespread, that *Nirvāṇa*, the *Summum Bonum* of Buddhism is synonymous with total annihilation of being. Rightly understood, *Nirvāṇa* implies the *going out* or *cooling* of the three fires of Desire which are Lust, Ill-will and Stupidity. When these have been extinguished, or become *cool*, or, esoterically considered, are transmuted into Purity, Goodwill, and Wisdom thereby dispelling Ignorance (Skt. Avidyā), there dawns the Perfect Knowledge of Buddhahood. The great

> scholars of Buddhist India who supervised the translations for the Sanskrit or religious lore now embodied in the Tibetan canonical books of the Mahāyāna Scriptures understood this subtle sense of the term *Nirvāṇa*, and translated it into the Tibetan as "The Sorrowless State" (Mya-ṅam-med).[7]

Thus, although the Tibetan language has inherent in it the potential for interpreting a Buddhism unique to Tibet, the unique aspect of Tibetan Buddhism has not been recognized by many scholars, because they have not noticed that the Tibetans had something to say in their translations, and further, because they have viewed the Tibetan language as a mere representation of Indian Buddhism.

There is no doubt that the Tibetan language was modelled after the Sanskrit language, but this is no ground for assuming that the Tibetan texts are merely mediums for expressing Indian thought. This contention is as absurd as assuming that the Japanese have nothing more to say because they have borrowed the whole system of Chinese characters from the Chinese!

II. *A Certain Consistency in the Translation of Major Technical Terms.*

On the foundation that the Sanskrit language has a special status among the oriental languages which deal with Buddhism, scholars have made an investigation into the consistency in the translations of major technical terms from the Sanskrit into Tibetan. Their conclusion has been, generally speaking, that Tibetan texts are "verbatim" translations of the Sanskrit texts.

Representative of this position are statements made by S. Yamaguchi, D.T. Suzuki, and S. Lévi.

S. Yamaguchi states:

> Under the circumstance and in consideration of the time factor, there was no alternative but to invent a purely artificial language, rather after the fashion of original Sanskrit. Then in collaboration with Indian Scholars, the Tibetan translators simply made a verbatim translation. This accounts for the fact that the translated Texts are for the most part, faithful copies of Sanskrit originals.[8]

D.T. Suzuki states:

> However, in the case of the Tibetan Tripiṭaka, it was rather different for the translation from the original Sanskrit was done verbatim and the words chosen for translation were well unified. The above mentioned factors

> make the Tibetan Tripiṭaka easily restorable to the original Sanskrit texts.[9]

And finally, S. Lévi states:

> Pour combler tant bien que mal cette douloureuse lacune, je me décidai à en restaurer le texte sanscrit d'après la version tibétaine, assuré contre les écarts excessifs par la fidélité littérale des traducteurs tibétains.[10]

In each case, the implication is that, since the Tibetan translations are "faithful copies", "verbatim translations", or "fidélité littérale des traducteurs tibétains", these Tibetan texts make it possible to "restore" or "reconstruct" the *original* Sanskrit texts.

However, as pointed out previously, Tibetan texts, even those found in the Tibetan Tripiṭaka, are more than mere "verbatim" translations. Despite a certain consistency in the translation of major technical terms, this is no indication of a "computerized" translation technique. The Tibetans have added their own views to the development of Buddhism in Tibet which gave it its unique characteristic and which, therefore, *must not* be understood by returning everything back to Sanskrit.

It must be pointed out at this time that I am not suggesting that translation from Tibetan into Sanskrit is impossible. On the contrary, I firmly believe that Tibetan texts can be translated into any language; but the claim that such a translation is a "restoration" or "reconstruction" of the original Sanskrit text is an assumption, first, that all Tibetan texts must be translations from the Sanskrit, and secondly, that the mere translation into Sanskrit gives that translation (and translator) a mark of difference from, say, translations into English.

Moreover, to those who will insist that on the basis of the consistency in the translation of major technical terms, a "reconstruction" or "restoration" is possible, I present the following questions:

(1) The Tibetan text to Chandrakirti's *Prasannapadā*, Chapter XX, K. 21, reads:

/ 'bras-bu ngo-bo-nyid yod-na /

/ rgyus-ni ci-zhig bskyed-par 'gyur /

/ 'bras-bu-ngo-bo-nyid med-na /

/ rgyus-ni ci-zhig bskyed-par 'gyur // 21 //

de-la 'bras-bu gang-zhig no-bo-nyid-kyis yod-pa rang-bzhin-gyis bdog-pa de-ni yang mi-skyes ste / yod-pa'i-phyir bum-pa yod bzhin-no // 'bras-bu ngo-bo-nyid-kyis med-pa gang yin-pa de yang rgyus bskyed-pa ma-yin te / ngo-bo-nyid-kyis yod-pa ma-yin-pa'i-phyir bong-bu'i-rwa bzhin-no //

(P. ed., Vol. 98, p. 62.3.7-8)

The sanskrit text (Poussin ed. p. 404) reads:

phalaṁ svabhāva-sadbhūtaṁ kiṁ hetur janayiṣyati /
phalaṁ svabhāvāsadbhūtaṁ kiṁ hetur janayiṣyati // 21 //

tatra yat phalaṁ svabhāvena sadbhūtaṁ svabhāvena vidyamānaṁ tan na punar janyate vidyamānatvāt / vidyamāna-ghaṭavat / yad api svabhāvenāsadbhūtaṁ phalaṁ, tad api hetur na janayati svabhāvenāsadbhūtatvāt, khara-viṣāṇavat //

Now, if the Tibetans translated verbatim, why is there one instance in which *svabhāva* is translated *rang-bzhin*, whereas in all other instances, it is translated *ngo-bo-nyid?* And why is the one instance of *vidyamāna* translated by *bdog-pa* and all other instances by *yod-pa?*

(2) Also, if the Tibetan translations were "faithful copies", then why do we not find consistency in the use of certain verb forms and negative particles? For example, with respect to verb forms, we find such examples as follows:

The Tibetan used the term *sems* to translate *citta, sems-pa* to translate *cetanā*, but use *sems-can* or *sems-dpa'* to translate *sattva*. Now, if they were "faithful copies", one would expect to find *sems-can* a translation of *cittin* or *cittavant* (See Whitney, 1230 and 1233) and *sems-dpa'* a translation of *citta-sūra* or *citta-vīra*. In other words, one would expect to find the same verb root in the Sanskrit form. Now, looking at this from the Sanskrit, we would expect *sattva* to be translated *yod-pa nyid,* if the Tibetans were so literal in their translation. Also, we often come across such a term as *sems-nyid*. Usually, this term, although composed of two elements *sems* and *nyid,* is understood as a unit. However, in most Tibetan-Sanskrit Indexes and Dictionaries, we do not find this term, although in Tibetan-Tibetan it appears as a single entry. If all Tibetan terms were "faithful copies", why is it that we do not find such an important word listed outside of Tibetan-Tibetan dictionaries?

With respect to negative particles, we find the following pecularities:

> We find that the Tibetan term *ma-rig-pa* is a translation of the Sanskrit term *avidyā*. Here the Tibetans have understood the negative particle *'a-'* in a passive sense; ie., something which was, is no longer the case. We find that the Tibetan term *bdag-med* is a translation of *anātman*. In this case, the Tibetans have understood the *'an-'* as an absolute negation. And finally, we find that *rig-byed ma-yin* is a translation of *avijñapti*. Here, the Tibetans have understood the *'a-'* in the sense that something is not the case.

If Tibetan texts are "faithful copies", why do we find such particularities.

Now, the claim that, through such methods, a supposedly lost text can be restored back to its "original" Sanskrit is not only naive, but has certain frustrating consequences. A case in point is a statement found in Sujitkumar Mukhopadyaya's work, the *Nairātmyaparipṛcchā*. In the *Foreword* of that work, Bhattacharya wrote:

> The original Sanskrit text of the *Nairātmyaparipṛcchā* was supposed to have been lost and just when . . . Mr. Sujitkumar Mukhopadhyaya was going to the press with his reconstruction in Sanskrit of the treatise from the Tibetan version, the Octo-Decem. number of the *Journal Asiatique* came to his hand, containing a paper by Prof. Lévi in which the original text . . . was published. A good deal of the value of the restoration of the text . . . has been thus lost. . . .[11]

I do not deny the value of such exercises for the development of one's skill in Sanskrit, but the so-called restoration had been given the status of a "great accomplishment" in the past simply because scholars have refused to give Tibetans credit where it was due. Scholars still believe that any work, which does not account for Sanskrit equivalents is not worthy of future investigation. When I read a review of *Mind in Buddhist Psychology*, a book published jointly by Dr. Guenther and myself, I found that the reviewer thought that much value was lost because we did not include Sanskrit terms although the text we translated was a Tibetan "original" and in spite of the fact that we had given all of the technical terms in Tibetan. Another person told me that the text was un-intelligible, because there were no Sanskrit equivalents given. If the Tibetan language was merely a reflection of the Sanskrit, these reviewers who believe and claim as much, should have no problems returning everything back into Sanskrit.

Thus, these arguments put forth by scholars who claim a "divine" status for Sanskrit and firmly feel that they can translate "with fidelity to the well-established Sanskrit-Tibetan correspondences"[12] are no more than *ex post facto* arguments; they apply only in cases where both the Sanskrit texts and a Tibetan translation are in existence and where the literalness of the latter can be established by comparative methods.

III. *A Belief that Anything Connected with Tibetan Buddhism Has its Origin in India*

Because of the special status given to the Sanskrit language, and as a consequence to anything Indian, by Buddhist scholars, Tibetan Buddhism has been forced to take a secondary position in Buddhology. The reason for this lies, together with the nature of Sanskrit, in the further fact that Tibetan political events have been considered to be historically valid, at least up to the present. According to some historians, the debate at bSam-yas, which is said to have taken place in 792-794, resulted from an unrest regarding the teaching between those who followed Śāntira-kṣita and those who followed the Chinese Ho-shang. Kamalaśīlā, a disciple of Śāntirakṣita was invited to Tibet to defend the Indian interpretation. About this, Tucci states:

> According to the Tibetan sources, Śāntirakṣita, usually known by the Tibetans as the Bodhisattva and the mk'an-po, the (first) abbot of bSam yas, had anticipated that the heresey - such was to him the Dhyāna school - would have spread so widely in Tibet as to endanger the right understanding of the doctrine; therefore on the point of death he had recommended in his will that, should the situation grow worse, his pupil, Kamalaśīla was to be invited. When new troubles arose, Ye-śes dbaṅ-po (Jñānendra), viz. one of the seven Tibetans who, as tradition would have us believe, were then properly ordained (sad mi bdun) . . . was insistently asked by the king to start the controversy with the Mahāyāna Hva san. Jñānendra refused to appear before the king and only when he was threatened with death if he insisted on his refusal, he came to the court to remind the king of the promise he had made Śāntirakṣita.[13]

It is said that this debate gave occasion to the writing of the three *Bhāvanākrama* texts and historians up to the present would have us believe that the Indian view won over the Chinese one at this debate. However, Yoshiro Imaeda's recent research into Tibetan documents found in Tun-huang concerning the council in question suggests that "they make no mention of a face-to-face confrontation between the two masters, Chinese and Indian."[14] Thus, on the basis of Imaeda's investigation, ". . . one cannot help but conclude that the famous confrontation between the two masters was not a historical fact, but a legend invented by later Tibetan historians."[15] If Imaeda's conclusion be accepted, then we can view the bSam-yas debate rather lightly as another means to emphasize the psuedo-importance of the Indian tradition in the development of Tibetan Buddhism.

The bSam-yas debate has been an important factor for the predominance of the Indian interpretation. In conjunction with this debate, we must question the possible influences into Tibet from countries other than India. Because, in one sense, the bSam-yas debate was so important in establishing the Indian interpretation, "there arose a tendency to claim as the authentic form of Buddhism only the development of Buddhist thought that was reflected in works of which a Sanskrit or other Indian language original had been available, which in practice meant that everything non-Indian was no longer recognized as 'Buddhistic'."[16] This meant that there was a "tendency to shut off the rNyingma tradition, although it is still very much alive . . ."[17] and also that there was a bias that all knowledge came into Tibet. H.V. Guenther states:

> Because of the geographical situation in Tibet, wherever we look we find that communication has come from all sides, but the trend has been to consider it as having come from India alone. It could just as well have been that India was not always the source of knowledge, but was also on the receiving end.[18]

CONCLUSION

Thus, in the light of the previous discussions, we can clearly see that there is a possibility for an indigenous Tibetan Buddhism - viz., the rNyingma tradition - without having to resort to only those texts which have an Indian background. Further, in view of such indigenous systems, Tibetan Buddhism must not be understood by converting everything back into Sanskrit. The texts must be understood in the language in which they were written - namely, Tibetan.

Buddhist scholarship has matured now to the point that it must go beyond the search for linguistic equivalents from one language to another. The value of our studies does not lie in the ability to "reconstruct" nor to "restore" the so-called "lost texts". It lies in making meaningful interpretations, albeit, faithful to whatever tradition we may be investigating for what that tradition stands. The language in which we make these interpretations can be Sanskrit as well as English.

To that end, we must be prepared to give up antiquated methods and cherished concepts which blind us from seeing what indigenous Tibetan materials have to offer. Erwin Schrodinger once wrote words of wisdom regarding the status of Science, but since it holds just as aptly for the future of Buddhist studies, I shall quote him in conclusion. He states:

> The quantum mechanics of today commits the error of maintaining concepts of the classical mechanics of points - energy, impulse, place, etc., - at the cost of denying to a system in a precisely determined state any definite value for their magnitudes. This shows how inadequate these concepts are. The concepts themselves must be given up, not their sharp definability.[19]

1 Alexander Csoma de Körös, *Tibetan English Dictionary* (New Delhi, Mañjuśrī Publishing House, 1973), p. v.
2 *Ibid.*, p. viii.
3 S.C. Das, *Contributions on the Religion and History of Tibet* (New Delhi, Mañjuśrī Publishing House, 1970), pp. 32-33.
4 See H.V. Guenther "Early Forms of Tibetan Buddhism", in *Crystal Mirror* (Emeryville, Dharma Publishing, 1974), Vol. III, pp. 80-92.
5 See for example, Bhikshu Sangharakshita, *A Survey of Buddhism* (Bangalore, The Indian Institute of World Culture, 1957), p. 418.
6 S.C. Das, *Tibetan English Dictionary* (Calcutta, Bengal Secretariat Book Depot, 1902; reprinted 1960), p. xiii.
7 W.Y. Evan-Wentz, *Tibetan Yoga and Secret Doctrine* (London, N.Y., Toronto, Oxford University Press, 1958), pp. 7-8.
8 S. Yamaguchi, "Publication of the Peking Edition of the Tibetan Tripitaka", in a brochure introducing the Peking Edition of the Tibetan Tripitaka, p. 4.
9 D.T. Suzuki, "The Object of Publication of the Tibetan Tripitaka", in a brochure introducing the Peking Edition of the Tibetan Tripitaka, p. 1.
10 S. Lévi, *Vijñaptimātratāsiddhi, Deux Traités de Vasubandhu, Viṁśatikā (La Vingtaine) et Triṁśikā (La Trentaine)*, (Paris, Librairie Ancienne Honoré Champion, 1925), p. xiii.
11 S. Mukhopadhyaya, *Nairātmyaparipṛcchā* (Calcutta, Visva-Bharati Book Shop, Visva-Bharati Studies No. 4, 1931), see his Foreword.
12 Alex Wayman, "Short Reviews" Guenther H.: Buddhist Philosophy in Theory and Practice, *Kailash - A Journal of Himalayan Studies*, Vol. 1, No. 4, p. 341.
13 G. Tucci, *Minor Buddhist Texts* (Roma, Istituto Italiano Per Il Medio ed Estremo Oriente, 1958), p. 8.
14 Y. Imaeda, "Documents Tibétains de Touen-Houang Concernant Le Concile du Tibet", in *Journal Asiatique*, Tome CCLXIII, Fascicules 1 et 2, p. 146.
15 *Ibid.*, p. 146.
16 H.V. Guenther, *Op. cit.*, p. 81.
17 *Ibid.*, p. 81.
18 *Ibid.*, p. 82.
19 Erwin Schrodinger "Uber die Unanwendbarkeit der Geometrie im Kleinen" *Naturwisseuschaften*, Vol. 22 (1934), p. 519.

1. LA LANGUE DE YA'UDI

Description et classement de l'ancien parler de Zencirli dans le cadre des langues sémitiques du nord-ouest

PAUL EUGENE DION, O.P.

1974 509 pp.
ISBN 0-919812-01-5 $4.50 (paper)

STUDIES IN RELIGION / SCIENCES RELIGIEUSES
Revue canadienne / A Canadian Journal

Abonnements / Subscriptions

Abonnement personnel: $10.00 (quatre fascicules)
Abonnement pour les institutions: $15.00 (quatre fascicules)
Fascicule isolé: $4.00

Individual subscriptions: $10.00 (four issues)
Institutional subscriptions: $15.00 (four issues)
Individual issues: $4.00

ISSN 0008-4298

Tout chèque doit être fait à l'ordre de Wilfrid Laurier University Press.

Make cheques payable to Wilfrid Laurier University Press

WILFRID LAURIER UNIVERSITY PRESS
Wilfrid Laurier University
Waterloo, Ontario, Canada N2L 3C5